Going for
GROWTH

Going for GROWTH

A Guide to Corporate Strategy

Michael K Lawson

Published in association with
Moores and Rowland

Kogan Page

Acknowledgements

A fundamental concept may be the product of a single mind; a good book is rarely so. Thanks are due to a number of people whose skill, constructive criticism and encouragement improved the final product enormously: Bob Rabone, Geoff Taylor, Stephen Gruneberg and Len Lawson who all took considerable trouble over reading and commenting on the early drafting; Lynne Drake and Iris Gardner whose inexhaustible patience and deft word processing skills coped with innumerable redrafting exercises. To all concerned, please accept my thanks.

First published in Great Britain in 1987
by Kogan Page Ltd, 120 Pentonville Road,
London N1 9JN

British Library Cataloguing in Publication Data

Lawson, Michael
  Going for growth: a guide to corporate
  strategy.
  1. Corporate planning
  I. Title
  658.4'012   HD30.28

  ISBN 1-85091-157-6

Typeset by Columns of Reading
Printed and bound in Great Britain by
Biddles Ltd, Guildford and King's Lynn

Contents

CONTENTS

Preface

If there is one feature that characterises the small business sector more than any other it is the tendency to manage from day to day, emphasising short-term decisions that have short-term consequences. Many smaller businesses faced with the need to survive in a competitive world consider time put aside for planning for the future a luxury they cannot afford. Correspondingly, a consistent feature noticeable in successful larger firms is that short-term decisions are taken in the context of consistent, carefully thought out long-term business policies.

Firms who survive and prosper are those who plan systematically and in conformity with longer-term goals. Such firms are invariably better managed and hence profitable. In these firms managers and staff alike are able to identify their goals clearly and do what is necessary for their achievement. It is perhaps not surprising that firms like this normally have a happy, well motivated staff. By contrast firms who cling to a 'crisis management' and 'fire-fighting' business philosophy usually suffer from low morale and high staff turnover, which is always visible to the customer.

I welcome Michael Lawson's book. It provides significant guidance for the small businessman on how to survive today and grow tomorrow. Increasingly, as the strategic approach is more widely practised, so will UK firms become more efficient and better placed *vis-à-vis* foreign competition.

DAVID TRIPPIER RD JP MP
Minister for Small Firms

Introduction

A tale of two companies

In the early 1970s a young inventor came up with the idea of a new product that was capable of revolutionising home maintenance. Not being a businessman, he decided that his skills would be better devoted to product development and he delegated the business side of the operation to some personal friends experienced in running their own business. Unusually, money was not a problem, and a small group of investors was brought together to back the project. Within a relatively short period of time it seemed as though all the ingredients for a successful business had been marshalled and high profitability was only just around the corner.

Yet the business never seemed to take off. Within a few years an inferior copy of the product had been produced which, by 1980, had achieved a degree of market acceptance. Even the name under which the business started trading had been hijacked – the proprietors had not got around to registering it or forming a limited company to protect it. Yet the business carried on, fuelled by the unquenchable enthusiasm of its proprietors. The potential was still vast, since the market penetration of the competitor was limited. Yet the actual breakthrough never seemed to come.

In 1985 the company sought the advice of management consultants in establishing the reasons for failure and finding a solution to the problem. The consultants' comments were: 'You have never established a long-term plan for your business. Having started with a good idea, you never decided where you wanted to take it. You could also have taken more care in protecting your product from competition. However, the potential is still there and the possibilities are still vast. You need to decide exactly what market need your product is trying to fulfil and consequently what

9

market you should be addressing. You are in danger of chasing too many possibilities and need to concentrate your efforts in a more limited number of directions. You must also consider the image that your product conveys by its packaging. But marketing alone is not enough; if you are to break through into a bigger league you must be certain of your ability to produce the product in quantity at an acceptable cost. You also need to be confident that your administrative arrangements are capable of handling the volume of trade that will arise. In summary, you need to aim at a target turnover and profitability you would like to achieve in, say, five years' time, establish how you intend to achieve it and what the implications of its achievement are for all areas of the business. In short, you need a corporate strategy.'

At around the same time as the inventor came up with his idea, some energetic employees of a bathroom accessories manufacturer decided they wanted to set up in business on their own. They planned the establishment of their company carefully, arranging the design of their first inexpensive and cautiously limited range before they formally set up in business. They were reasonably successful and went on to design and sell further ranges year by year, each one becoming a little more ambitious. However, in the late 1970s it became increasingly clear that the cheaper end of the market (the sector in which they were functioning) was in decline and that all manufacturers at this end would feel the pinch. The company took the strategic decision to introduce a new range of much higher quality merchandise aimed at the more stable upper end of the market. The new product was well received and each successive range penetrated further into the chosen market sector. Eventually the cheaper, lower quality product range was dispensed with altogether. By the mid-1980s the company was established as one of the foremost UK manufacturers in its field. It was in firm control of an international manufacturing and marketing operation and was running its own chain of retail outlets. Moreover, it had gone public at a valuation that made its proprietors multi-millionaires.

What lay at the root of this success story? The proprietors put it simply: 'We got it mostly right most of the time.' Behind the simple statement lay a business that had indeed got it mostly right. The product was popular and was delivered to the customer when he wanted it. The control systems of the company were so well developed that it was possible to cut wastage almost to nothing and to predict profitability months in advance. Enormous pains were taken to obtain and retain high quality staff in key positions who were energetically motivated by the proprietorial team. And of vital importance was the wholehearted commitment of the staff to the company that the proprietors were able to engender.

How had it been possible to get so much so right? Certainly the company had not, until a year before it went public, developed a written corporate strategy. But each step had been carefully planned, each decision carefully considered in the light of its impact on the rest of the business and the long-term future of the company. In the minds of the proprietors the strategy for success was clearly understood.

What this book is not

Both of these examples (and indeed, all those quoted in this book) are drawn from real-life situations. Only the industries and locations have been changed. They are quoted to illustrate the difference that planning can make in the running of a business, regardless of the industry it is in. There is an inclination among small businessmen to believe that planning is only for the big boys, that they themselves are too small to benefit from the planning process. When specialist terms like 'corporate strategy' are used and since most of the books on planning are written in highbrow Americanese for MBA students, the feeling is reinforced. At the other end of the scale, books explaining how to start a business (setting up a company, borrowing money etc) are numerous and their number needs no adding to (although anyone thinking of going into business should certainly read at least one of these) and it is not the intention of this book to duplicate material available elsewhere.

Having decided that it is your intention to go into business, and in some cases having done it and actually survived for a while, what next? The truth of the matter is that most businessmen find it hard enough making the time to think about next year let alone devising a masterplan for the following three or four. Yet it remains stubbornly (and perhaps unfortunately) true that very little real success can ever be achieved in the long term without careful planning and constant monitoring of actions to ensure that they are in keeping with stated long-term goals. Being in business is like fighting a war. Armies gain victories through the formulation and execution of clear strategies where fighting resources are deployed in pursuit of defined aims. Not every soldier is in the right place at the right time. Not every engagement with the enemy is successful. But merely to react to the way the enemy deploys his forces and so give him the upper hand spells certain defeat.

The concept is no different in the manufacture of a motor car. Without planning, the components would not be available in the right place at the right time in the right quantities. The order of assembly would be inefficient and haphazard and essential parts would left left out. Yet while most businessmen can see the need for planning in the manufacturing process, the need for the same degree of planning in the business as a whole is less clearly understood. But if the point has not been sufficiently clearly stated already, let it be summarised:

> To be successful in business over a period of years you must have a goal. Planning and the application of strategy are of fundamental importance in both the achievement of that goal and the control of the business while *en route* to it. In this context the size of the business is immaterial. From the largest international conglomerate down to the smallest one-man business, establishing targets and planning for their achievement is essential to success.

The overriding purpose of this book is, therefore, to make you think and to make you think strategically. Read it because you are tired of firefighting and crisis management. Read it because you want to determine your own future and not be run by events.

What is corporate strategy?

Despite the expensive wrapping paper in which it is usually packaged the definition is, in fact, quite straightforward. Corporate strategy is the process of defining a route for getting a business from where it is now to where you want it to be at a stated point in the future.

To emphasise the point, take as an example the way the UK economy has moved over the last ten years. A significant number of large companies, former bastions of UK industry, have either gone under or have come close to doing so. However, still more have survived. The ones that have adjusted best to the recession are those that developed a strategy to meet it head on. Some have even used it to their advantage, trimming down the unprofitable areas of their businesses within the guidelines of a clearly defined strategy for rejuvenating themselves over a period of time. Those who, during the previous 20 years of affluence, had grown too complacent to plan a route through the recession increasingly risked business death through corporate failure. As the recession lessens the large-firm sector is emerging both fitter and more aware of the practical value of corporate planning.

At the other end of the size scale, increasing emphasis has been placed by successive governments on the small-firm sector as an engine of future economic growth, the philosophy apparently being that from little acorns mighty oaks do grow. While estimates indicate that business start-ups are taking place at an ever increasing rate, statistics suggest that only 10 per cent of new businesses may survive the first five years. By contrast, among franchise operations where corporate plans are nearly always established before the new business commences, the success rate is said to be nearer 90 per cent. It seems highly likely that the small firms that are going to survive are the ones that plan their future growth most carefully.

The conclusion is obvious: experience throughout the economy proves the value of planning for any business regardless of its size or activity. To make the process work successfully you need to define and employ the two aspects of planning that together make up the strategic approach to running a business:

Strategic planning sets out the overall direction that the proprietor wishes his business to take over that period. But on its own it isn't enough. While you need to be aware of the long term and define overall parameters, doing so mustn't put out of focus the equally important requirements of planning in more detail over the shorter term and giving practical effect to those plans.

Tactical planning (sometimes called operational planning), therefore, is a procedure for defining more limited objectives within sub-divisions or aspects of a business over a shorter time.

While for the business as a whole it is important to develop an overall strategy for, say, a five-year period, it is also necessary to develop shorter-term plans for each aspect of the business (marketing, production, finance etc) whose achievement is regularly monitored to ensure that constant and regular progress is being made towards the overall goal. Devising a full corporate

13

strategy for a company must involve both strategic and tactical planning to ensure success. Throughout the rest of this book, therefore, the term 'corporate strategy' will be taken to refer to the dual process of:

1. Long-term planning to define where the business is going.
2. Short-term planning and budgeting for each functional division of the business to define the intermediate targets that must be achieved to ensure arrival at the longer-term destination.

In essence then, this book sets out to explain the necessary steps involved in designing and implementing a corporate strategy. At this stage it will aid clarity to set out the points that will be developed more fully in the following chapters.

Why plan?

Other than for the reasons already stated (to reach the targets set) there are at least three clearly distinguishable reasons for undertaking a corporate planning exercise:

- to avoid failure;
- to ensure the adoption of common aims by everyone in the business;
- to measure achievement on a continuing basis.

Where does planning start?

The beginning of the planning period is now. But you will be able to set reasoned and realistic targets only when you have properly understood the organisation's present position. In this context you will need to consider all aspects of the business, but particularly:

- financial factors such as turnover and profit;
- marketing methods and markets;
- the range and quality of products produced;
- the key personnel and staffing of the organisation;
- the control systems employed.

Where does planning end?

Once you have established a clear understanding of where the business is starting from, deciding what it can grow into becomes

14

a much more straightforward task. You must set financial and non-financial goals for each aspect of the business and determine a suitable time-scale for the plan. In addition, you need to define appropriate yardsticks for measuring progress.

Which route to get there?

Having established the present condition and status of the company and defined appropriate targets, the actual means of getting from A to B need to be determined. There are at least four main possibilities, all of which may be used during the period of the plan if appropriate:

- growth of existing activities (the most obvious, but with far-reaching implications for marketing, organisation, personnel and information systems);
- diversification (but how well will new activities integrate with old?);
- acquisition of other businesses (but why is the vendor selling?);
- internal re-organisation (how to raise profit without raising turnover).

What to do on arrival?

The danger of emphasising a three- or five-year target is that people tend not to see beyond it. It is necessary to start planning for the next period well before the current one ends – and, also, what happens if the company does not achieve its targets?

If you have never undertaken it before, the corporate planning process may not be an easy one. It demands time which could be spent on more immediate and apparently more urgent problems. It will call for objectivity concerning the strengths and weaknesses of a business that you, the proprietor, may love like your own child. It may call for expense if it is necessary to call in outsiders to help develop the strategy. It will certainly call for the discipline of regular monitoring if it is to be used properly once established.

However, if the time, objectivity, expense and discipline are devoted, the chances of success will be increased many times over. The change in attitude to your business that the process will bring to you as proprietor will bear fruit in the management of that business. And the time devoted to participation in the planning

15

process by key staff will be fully rewarded by the commitment to achieving corporate goals that such participation will engender.

Chapter 1
Why Plan?

When the benefits of planning are fully perceived and the dangers of failing to plan properly understood, the best answer to the question 'Why plan?' will be obvious: 'Because no serious businessman can honestly afford not to'. The four key reasons for adopting a corporate strategy have been stated as:

1. To reach a destination.
2. To avoid failure.
3. To ensure the adoption of common aims by everyone in the business.
4. To measure achievement.

To reach a destination

In the mid 1970s a 28-year-old computer software expert decided to set himself the goal of becoming a millionaire by the time he was 40. He knew that if his goal was ever to become reality he would have to plan its achievement. He reasoned that since his expertise lay in computer software it was through that activity that he was most likely to achieve his aims. His intention was to write a suite of accounting programs applicable to a specific sector of industry and capable of running on a variety of micro-computers. But the development costs of such a package would be high, and he would be unlikely to obtain finance for the sum he needed. Instead, therefore, he decided to delay the development of the package and concentrate on a cash generating activity – a computer bureau. The bureau was successful and the considerable amount of cash generated was kept in the company and used to fund the development of the accounting packages. The packages became some of the most respected products in their sector and in

17

time also became highly cash-generative. The entrepreneur went on to sell a stake in his business to a city institution at a price that valued the business at several million pounds. By the age of 37 he had achieved his goal, three years in advance of the targeted date. The process was not without its setbacks and not everything the company attempted was successful, but the moral of the story is clear – the target was achieved through careful planning, foresight and constant attention to monitoring development towards the goal.

To avoid failure

To some businessmen, simply being in business is reward enough – becoming wealthy is not a particular goal. But no matter how modest the aim, the dramatic failure rate in the small-business sector makes proper planning essential. At the other end of the size scale, failure can creep up on the largest business if it is not purposeful and if it does not monitor progress. It is the definition of a goal and checking progress towards it that makes management constantly aware of the need to avoid starting on the slippery slope down to corporate death.

Around 1980 a long established, medium-sized, family-run service company in the engineering industry started to manifest difficulties. Problems were blamed on the decline in the industry and market penetration by large national competitors, but the real root of the problem was that the management had lost direction, and consequently the company had no aim. By 1985 the problem had become so acute that receivership was a serious possibility. Eventually the company was saved through the intervention of outside consultants. Salvation lay in motivating the management into believing that the company had a future and in designing a recovery plan. The plan covered all aspects of the business and set specific financial and non-financial targets together with dates for their achievement. The company survived through the development of a strategy to avoid failure. If it had undertaken a planning exercise five years earlier and monitored its own development, the whole of the problem could have been avoided.

To ensure the adoption of common aims by everyone in the business

Even if the proprietor has not planned the future of the business, the people working for it will normally have planned theirs. The problem arises when they see their interests being served by actions that are not necessarily in the interests of the company. Even when employees attempt to act in the interests of the company, unless corporate goals have been specified they may be adopting attitudes that are incompatible or may not serve the company optimally. The solution is to harness the efforts of employees to clearly stated corporate goals by ensuring that those goals also serve the interests of the individuals within the organisation. The technical term is 'goal congruence' and it is generated by involving key employees in the life of the business and by ensuring that the success of the company results in those who are responsible for that success being properly rewarded and being recognised as responsible. More of this later.

In 1980 a small manufacturer in Kent went into liquidation, despite having a lucrative contract to supply a national retail chain. It had been fraught with problems for a considerable period and there was no one reason for its failure. However, during the 12 months preceding its demise, the marketing director had been quoting to potential customers not only on behalf of the company, but on his own behalf as well. Needless to say, his personal quotes were more competitive than those he gave on behalf of the company! The moral of the story? Had the company developed a corporate plan and had the marketing director been involved in its development and been offered rewards geared to its achievement he would have been more likely to have seen his own interests as being bound up with the success of the company. The point is often made that a company's most important resources are its people. It is unfortunate that when daily practicalities press in, their value is all too easily forgotten.

To measure achievement

For most proprietors, the purpose of engaging in business is to make a profit. Periodically it is necessary to measure what has been achieved. But it is meaningless simply to state 'we made £50,000 profit last year' unless there is some kind of standard against which to measure that achievement. Comparisons with historical records ('we made 25 per cent more than last year') or with others in the same industry (we did better than 75 per cent of the competition) can be useful, but they are not sufficiently objective – there may be good reasons why the company should expect to do better (or worse!) than the competition or than it did last year. The establishment of a corporate plan from which tactical annual budgets are derived gives a more objective standard against which to measure performance (we did 15 per cent better than we expected to this year, and the reasons were . . .). So long as a degree of flexibility is built into the plan, account can also be taken of changing circumstances when the time comes to declare the verdict of success or failure.

In 1983 two individuals were given the opportunity to acquire a specialist engineering company in the north of England. To finance the purchase it was necessary to raise venture capital, and to do so a corporate plan was developed. The plan was sufficiently attractive and realistic to persuade a city institution to invest and the financial targets embodied in the plan were used to measure the success of the new management in running the company. It was agreed that the level of success achieved would finally determine the cost to the company of the venture capital raised. The outcome was that the buyers of the business regularly did better than they expected and were able to prove it by reference to previously established targets in the corporate plan. Consequently, the price of the finance was reduced.

Between them these four points encompass most of the reasons why it's important to undertake the planning process.

Now, if that's the why, what about the how? If you decide to undertake a corporate plan (and it's rare for a business not to benefit from doing so), be aware that you're embarking on a time-consuming and sometimes painful process. Don't let the effort drag you down, because the long-term benefits of completing the process will be enormous. However, there are some ground rules which you can usefully employ, and to these attention will now be turned.

Chapter 2
Starting at the Beginning

Rules of the road to planning

Everything is more important than something that's difficult to do. And when time is at a premium, as it is for most businessmen, it's easy to find an activity that prevents the start of a large, difficult, important project. Unfortunately, the initial stages of a corporate planning exercise can be both difficult and unpleasant; difficult because it's hard to know where to start, and unpleasant because during the first stage of the process most people learn a number of home truths that it's usually more comfortable to ignore. Corporate planning must really start with a thorough understanding of every aspect of the business, warts and all. If, on completion of stage one of the planning process, you don't find any system that needs changing, any policy capable of further development or any member of staff who is being underused, congratulations – you've achieved a first in business history!

The first property of inertia (not getting started) is a problem that needs to be tackled, and is best handled by gritting your teeth and getting down to planning a full analysis of the business. The second property of inertia (once started, things keep going) can be quite useful, though – once you get started, and as the momentum builds up there is a tendency to continue (even at the times when you're inclined to question the benefit of the process). So Rule 1 is:

Get started now or you'll never get started at all.

It doesn't matter where in your financial year you are, it doesn't matter how important that outstanding phone call is (even if your wife is waiting on the line), dictate a memo to your secretary now to arrange a board meeting with one item on the agenda: getting the corporate planning exercise under way by arranging a written analysis of where the company is now. You're too small to have a board? Call a meeting of your key staff instead but whatever you do don't try to do it on your own. If there is no one else to call on, involve a management consultant or your accountant.

Why shouldn't you do it on your own? Because the boss is the least objective of all people about his business. Every managing director knows he's got the best in the world, whether it's company, product, staff or market – and usually it's all of them. Unfortunately, managing directors tend to be short on objectivity. In addition, there is no point in your compiling a one-man corporate plan based on your impressions of the company and then expecting your staff to fulfil your targets. They will never feel morally or practically committed unless they have had a hand in setting them, and if they are going to be involved they should be involved from the start.

One example will suffice. The chief executive of a successful Welsh crafting company was a dominant figure, respected and a little feared by his management team. He was quick to appreciate the value of formal corporate planning, but being autocratic in his management style, he decided to develop the strategy single-handed. The result was a written document containing targets, issued to managers with the instruction to meet those targets. Unfortunately, because their detailed knowledge had not been used in setting them, these goals were less than realistic and the managers had little personal commitment to their achievement.

Rule 2 is, therefore, fairly obvious:

Involve key staff in analysing the present situation.

A lot of this presupposes a company large enough to find separate individuals responsible for each functional division of the business. But one of the purposes of this text is to demonstrate the value of corporate strategy to the small company. Reference was made above to the possibility of using management consultants if you have no one available (or indeed if the required skills or time are unavailable) to ensure that the plan is a corporate effort. Two points need to be spelled out at this stage if you are in such a position and are contemplating such a step:

1. Do not make the consultant responsible for certain functional areas while you personally handle others. Remember that when the exercise finishes and the consul-

tant is not around anymore it's Muggins who must bear primary (or full) responsibility for the implementation of the plan. You will not be able to do so if there are large gaps in your knowledge because you did not participate adequately in all areas of the plan.

Instead use him as a sounding board for your ideas on all areas of the business, and expect him to come up with his own ideas to feed into the plan.

2. Choose your consultant with care! No one has exclusive rights to the term 'management consultant' and you don't have to be qualified in any field to call yourself one. You must therefore assure yourself of the competence of the individual or firm chosen before committing yourself. One solution to this problem is to use a nationally known firm, but it can be an expensive solution and not one that will necessarily guarantee you end up with an individual within the firm who has expertise in corporate planning. Business strategy is a relatively new area of activity for many consultancy firms. Make sure they are not gaining their experience at your expense. The best solution is to ask for a recommendation from someone you trust – your accountant or bank manager – and if in doubt ask for references from satisfied clients, preferably in your line of business. While we're on the subject, professional expertise never comes cheap, so always ask for a quotation of the maximum figure payable for the exercise and, when you recover from fainting, consider as objectively as possible what you're getting for the fee. When the time comes to pay the bill, if you've been quoted a maximum figure, unforeseen circumstances aside, it's not unreasonable to expect the fee to be somewhat less than the maximum quoted.

Rule 3 is equally straightforward:

Write down everything that is relevant.

Do not try to rely on memory, consensus or any other substitute – it won't work. Make notes of discussions, interviews, calculations, brainstorming sessions and meetings. When you get to the end of this first analytical stage of the exercise, draw up agreed formal conclusions; they will take you a long way down the road to deciding where you are going.

Mentioned in Chapter 1 was a family-run engineering services company that nearly went under for want of a corporate plan. Now there can be many points of strength in the family company not least of which is trust, but one of the disadvantages of such an entity is that family members are so used to seeing each other over the dinner table that they find it difficult to be formal with one another across the board-room table and, indeed, this was one problem that this particular company faced. Formality is something that comes much more easily in the large impersonal organisation than the small enterprise whose strength lies in the personal touch. Yet lack of an adequate degree of formality will spell death to the planning process.

Rule 4 is the corollary of all that has gone before:

> Don't let the planning process, its formality and the length of time it requires for completion, become an excuse for failing to do what clearly needs to be done now.

For instance, an examination of your debtor position may lead to the conclusion that something needs to be done about bringing cash in more quickly. As far as corporate strategy is concerned the point to note is that a formal debt collection procedure should be designed and implemented. Noting the need as part of stage one of the planning process should not be used as an excuse for failing to get on the telephone *now* to late payers. Rule 4 can be expressed another way: Do it now – and if you really can't, make a written note to do it tomorrow.

Having set the ground rules for the 'where are we now?' stage of the exercise it becomes a little more difficult to detail where you go next. The aim is to arrive at a full analysis of all areas of the business. Necessarily, any categories defined here will be of limited application to your own company and there will undoubtedly be others that are relevant to you. The only satisfactory way to proceed is to define all those areas applicable to your business and to assess its current status within those categories. The first item to be discussed at that initial board meeting could usefully be the appropriate categories into which to divide the business.

Another matter is relevant at this stage; while it has already been stated that the managing director (or chief executive or whatever – he is still the boss whatever he is called) should not write the corporate plan on his own, it is equally important that too many fingers do not get into the pie at the same time. If the board is quite large, a team (say, three) should be established to co-ordinate progress through the planning exercise. The managing director should chair the team and other key personnel should be drafted in from time to time as their functional expertise and areas of responsibility become relevant. At all costs do not use the sub-committee approach as an excuse to exclude others – all key personnel should be involved in the plan at some point during the three key stages of:

- establishing where you are now;
- deciding where you want to go;
- determining a strategy for getting there.

Sets and subsets

If a thorough analysis of the business is to be conducted it is important to adopt a categorised approach. But a word of warning – never take functional categories of the business to the point where demarcation disputes arise. In a well run company all areas of responsibility should and will overlap. If a given person is keen to take responsibility for a given activity it is usually unwise to deny the request on grounds of functional definitions alone. Hence there will always be grey areas between marketing and finance, production and purchasing, personnel and premises. So long as responsibility can be allocated amicably let it be done on the adage 'a volunteer is worth ten pressed men'. But if an individual is evidently empire building and creating dissatisfaction at any level as a result, it is vitally important to get to the root of the problem quickly. Very commonly there is a lack of goal congruence, with the culprit seeing his own successful future as lying somewhere other than in the success of the organisation as a whole.

If a company is large enough to be subdivided functionally already, the existing divisions might be appropriate categories within which to examine the business:

- Marketing and sales
- Production
- Purchasing
- Personnel
- Administration
- Finance

Such categories may also be a useful starting point if you are too small to be using such divisions already. From these internal categories direct your attention outwards – much of the analysis will be undertaken with one eye on the competition, hence you should analyse your position in the context of the market and more general environment in which you are functioning. Here the category is referred to as:

- Contextual

From here look to activities that go on within the business itself that are not adequately defined within the above. If you undertake (or ought to undertake) substantial research and development a further appropriate category worthy of analysis might be:

- Developmental

Thereafter, you may be aware of certain problems before you start which could benefit from analysis quite separately from the above. In the example of W A Webb quoted at the end of this book a series of known problems were identified around which a complete one-year plan was developed, not least of which was constraint on office space. This particular problem was analysed separately from all other aspects of the business. Had it received less detailed attention under a more general category, it might not have been resolved so successfully.

Having established appropriate categories within which to analyse the present state of the business, the first major task is ready to be addressed: defining and specifying the yardsticks by which the business will be described. The committee approach to the task, though probably the best available, can result in the slight disadvantage of all members looking in embarrassment at each other over the board-room table, wondering what to do next – except of course for the smart Alec who's worked it all out already just to prove to the MD that he is one up on his peers (or perhaps he is trying to show the chairman that the MD's due for early retirement!). More seriously, the problem can be quite acute in the company that has never undertaken corporate planning before, particularly the informal family company. The moral of the story is: define the categories first, then send the relevant people away to define the most appropriate yardsticks and questions before ever you start to look for answers.

Going back to those typical categories mentioned above, it's possible here to raise only some of the general questions that might be applicable to most businesses. Careful thought by those to whom responsibility has been delegated should lead to questions (and hopefully answers!) more pertinent to specific circumstances that apply to your business.

Financial

No apology is necessary for starting this analysis with financial parameters. If you're looking for a means of describing a company in broad-brush terms, once you've defined the area of activity it's in, financial parameters are problably the most natural yardsticks – 'We're manufacturers of paper bags turning over £2 million per year' or 'We're a small fashion retail operation turning over £800,000 from two locations.'

The point of analysing the company is to define it from as many different perspectives as possible. Thus, the obvious first financial questions are:

1. What is the company's present turnover?
2. What is its present net profitability?

(*Note*: The profitability is most aptly defined before appropriations on profit of any kind – pension contributions, salaries above market rate etc. For a number of reasons, and often to maximise tax-efficient use of profits, the bottom line in the financial accounts will not truly define the profitability of the company. Thus, if directors' salaries are three times as high as it would cost to employ the same directors commercially, add back two-thirds to profit in arriving at the 'where we are now' definition.)

These two questions are probably the easiest to answer and also give the basis for the most general objectives that will be established in the corporate plan. But the full range of financial yardsticks is large, and it is important to select those that are most appropriate to the company itself. The following are examples of some that might be relevant.

3. What is the contribution (as a rule of thumb use the gross profit) of each product towards overhead and net profitability?

Take the example of a toy manufacturer in north London faced with the opportunity to expand output. He produced several different lines and the market could apparently absorb increased production of any of them. But he was faced with a space problem in the short term – he did not have the physical capacity to expand all lines. Question: Which product should he increase

27

output of? Normally the answer is to increase production of the item that makes the greatest contribution per unit to overhead and net profit. However, in a case like this, where there is a constraint on production, the better solution is to increase the output of the product whose contribution per unit of limiting factor is greatest. In practice, storage space was rented elsewhere, maximising available space for production, the calculations carried out and the relevant product went into increased production. Moral of the story: It is important to know what unit contribution your products are making. If you don't know, find out . . . now.

4. What is the true value of your assets (ie not book value)?

Go on, be honest. When was the last time you had a professional valuation carried out on your freehold? It may give a pleasant surprise to have one done – until you realise you've been underinsuring for the last X years. But seriously, do you have a sensible idea of the true asset net worth of the business? If not, the start of a corporate planning exercise is a fairly good time to find out.

5. What are the true liabilities of the company?

OK, so you probably a have a better idea of this one in pure numerical terms. Nevertheless be a little more imaginative and get your money's worth out of the planning exercise – rank your liabilities by size of creditor. Can any of them effectively behave as a monopolist as far as you are concerned? For example, what would you do if your main supplier announced a 50 per cent price rise overnight? Full marks to those who have already arranged second sourcing. For those that haven't, do something about it now unless there is good reason not to. And if it's not possible to arrange dual sourcing what protective clauses do you have in the contract with that oh-so-vital supplier? What, no contract? It's time to think again.

6. What is your stock turnover ratio?
7. How many days' sales do you currently have in debtors?
8. How many days' purchases do you currently have in creditors?
9. Would it be worthwhile to take advantage of quantity discounts?

These questions are grouped together because, among others, they are the bread and butter of management accounting control. Being fundamental to the running of a business, the answers should be known already. But they are, nevertheless, relevant to the planning exercise, since any deficiencies they exhibit must be rectified as part of the process (see Appendix 3 for some relevant calculations).

10. What is the cash position of the company?

Cash is the life-blood of any business. Without the ability to generate cash, all the profitability in the world will be wasted. Questions 6 to 9 above essentially address various aspects of the working capital needed to run a business. But why ask them? Why, for example, are stock turnover and debtor days important? Answer, because cash tied up in stock and debtors is cash that is not in the bank. It's cash in the bank that pays the bills, finances growth and gives the proprietor his rewards, and without cash generation you won't have a business for very long.

Contextual

It was mentioned earlier that financial yardsticks offer probably the best broad-brush parameters available in defining a business, after you define its area of activity. Having sent the finance director away to draft the list of appropriate financial questions, it's time to sit down with the marketing director to look at the market context in which your business functions. It's important to draw the distinction between markets and marketing here, since although the latter is of key significance in the planned growth strategy of the company, it cannot be determined without a thorough understanding of the former. It seems to be fashionable to chide British industry for failure to market itself properly, yet very little mention ever seems to be made of the need to understand your market before you begin to establish a strategy for attacking it. It suffices to say that if you can't be bothered to define your market adequately, don't bother to establish a marketing policy.

Determine questions relevant to your unique circumstances, but bear in mind the following general matters:

1. What does the company define as its market?

You are not just manufacturers of widgets. You are producers of high quality, high priced, high margin widgets aimed at males in the 40-60 age group who devote at least 25 per cent of their spare time to widgetry. You are quite distinct from volume producers of

29

inferior quality widgets aimed at the more cost-conscious, younger end of the market. To overstate the point, your market is not the same as theirs, nor theirs yours. Without understanding the fundamental point that there is not one widget market but many, you can never hope to get your corporate strategy right.

No doubt enough has been said to make some readers go cold in the feet! If you don't have an adequate, specific definition of the market-place (or places, for the multi-product company) it's time to construct one. And if that means going out and finding why your products sell and to whom they sell, so be it, because that's what marketing planning is all about.

2.   What is the company's market share?
3.   What is its market ranking?

Again, these are essentially questions that define the market in which you function. If you have 5 per cent of the market as defined in question 1 and are first by size, you're playing in a wholly different arena than if you are one of ten companies that have 5 per cent in a market of which 50 per cent is held by the largest three firms. Define your place in the market with care – it will have far-reaching consequences for both the contextual target you go on to set yourself and the marketing policy implemented to get you to the target.

4.   How stable is the market?

Establishing the boundaries and concentration of the market amounts to only the very broadest definition. Probably more important are the qualitative aspects which are inevitably difficult to quantify. It may be relatively easy to place a figure on size of market and market shares. It will be less easy to quantify stability. Yet the latter is of vital significance for any long-term decisions you seek to take on the future of the company. A feel for the stability of the market can be gained by looking at the degree of brand loyalty that attaches to a product, the age of the market etc. Instability can arise from a number of sources, eg:

(a)   speed of development of products (eg high technology);
(b)   influence of fashion (clothes, shoes);
(c)   price sensitivity.

There are, in essence, only two ways to face the problem of instability:

- do something to stabilise your market share;
- get out, and into something more stable.

But more of such things later.

The environmental context in which a business functions is not restricted to its market-place. Of great interest is the nature of its supplier base and, in many cases, its physical location.

5. What is the nature of the company's supplier base?

Reference has already been made to the value of second sourcing in case of difficulty of supply of essential input materials. The key consideration is (as far as possible) never to get into the situation where external, possibly malign, influences can dictate the running of the business. There may, of course, be very good reasons for sticking closely to one good supplier, and relationships that take years to establish can be easily destroyed by the implementation of a single, inadequately considered policy. But the good supplier who wishes to maintain a relationship with you will understand the reasoning behind the policy if adequate steps are taken to communicate it.

6. What is the nature of the competition?

A proper understanding of the market-place in which you function has to go further than simply analysing the nature and intentions of potential purchasers. You also need to give considered attention to what the competition is up to – not so that you can copy it, but so that your own decisions can be taken in the light of the influences of their actions upon your environment. Additionally, competition analysis may enable you to identify gaps in the market that you are to exploit profitably.

Start by clarifying in your own mind who the competition are and which competitors are most relevant to you. If you service only one small segment of a large market, those firms that service the same segment will be most relevant. If you address a limited geographical market, you will be concerned with the competition in the local environment. But also bear in mind the impact that your intentions will have on existing and potential competitors. While at this stage you are not considering objectives and routes for getting to them, the strategy you adopt and the objectives you aim at could well be substantially influenced by their impact on your potential as well as your existing competitors. Gain a clear understanding of the wider competitive environment and you will

31

have an enhanced understanding on which to base the forth-coming decision-making process.

7. What is the significance of physical location?

To some businesses (eg mail order houses) physical location may be virtually immaterial. To others (eg retailers) it is of crucial importance. One way or another it is important to establish two matters: Is physical location of significance to your business? Are the premises that you currently occupy adequate in the context of the corporate strategy on which you now intend to embark? The case study of W A Webb, reprinted in Appendix 2, exemplifies one answer to the question: in this instance the location from which the company traded was not of vital significance. What was of more importance was that the company's recent rate of growth had been great enough to cause the physical premises to create a major constraint. This was so much the case that one of the main tenets to the one-year plan was incorporated to solve the space problem.

You probably don't need to know your strategic plan in detail to consider the adequacy of your premises. If the plan is to be directed towards causing the company to grow, the central question is whether the current premises will be adequate for the enlarged, new look entity and the corporate image it is trying to convey.

While on the subject, you may wish to give consideration to your premises ownership policy. There are two conflicting approaches here, each having its merits in the right circumstances. The main argument against buying rather than renting a building is cash flow. If it has to be bought with a loan, any particular building is likely to take twice as much cash out of the firm if bought than if rented, at least until the rent is reviewed (usually three-yearly). It can be done, but at the expense of draining cash – which the growing firm is short of. You're in business to manufacture widgets, not run a building, so leave it to those whose business is property. On the other hand is the view that property has not gone down in value in living memory, so it must be a good thing to own. On balance, ownership tends to be a good idea if your balance sheet can do with strengthening, if you have the capital or borrowing capacity available and if your expansion plans could not better use the funds committed to the property. However, you must always bear in mind the physical capacity of the building and the ease with which it could be disposed of when you start to outgrow it.

Internal

Having dealt with the questions that define the broad parameters
of your company and the market in which it functions you will
have begun to get a good feel for the corporate planning concept.
In addition you will have started to highlight some of the areas
where the company is deficient (eg ease with which financial
information can be produced, your understanding of the market-
place etc). It's now time to approach the more introspective parts
of the definitional exercise by looking in detail at the internal
structure of the company, and later (the most sensitive aspect of
all) personnel-related questions.

The easiest place to start is usually with the organisational
structure.

1. How do we divide the various activities that our company
   undertakes?

If you've grown along unstructured lines until now, you may have
no clearly defined structure at all, rather like a certain small
confectionery manufacturer in the Midlands. The company had
grown from entrepreneurial concept to turnover of several
millions without any recognisable structure at all emerging. There
was no buying department, no sales department and no finance
department; instead, all administrative staff were designated as
assistants to the MD. Worst of all, they all sat in one very large
open-plan office where he could keep an eye on them and monitor
how many times they left the room during the course of the day.
Needless to say, staff relations left a great deal to be desired. Of
more significance to the MD/owner was that the company was far
less profitable than it could have been given a sensible organisational structure. The point was quickly proved (much to his
chagrin) when the company was later sold to buyers with rather
more workable concepts of business structures and man-
management.

A number of systems of organisation are workable. Many
companies adopt the traditional functional approach (sales
department, finance department etc), but this is not to suggest that
such is the only workable system. The smaller company, in
particular, may not be in a position to organise along such lines,
and in the early days one person may wear many hats. One
question that you should always bear in mind, though, is whether
you're failing to define structure through an unwillingness to
delegate.

Of course, other structural arrangements may be appropriate. For the company that functions from more than one location, one appropriate definition is obvious. Similarly the company whose market is clearly defined geographically may well find it convenient to organise along the lines of Eastern Region, Western Region etc. In any event, having established the way you're currently doing it, keep to the maxim of 'write everything down' and draw up an organisation chart along the lines in Figure 1 on page 35. This may give some immediate pointers to areas ripe for improvement.

Having established the skeleton of the business it's time to look in more detail at some of the other key internal features.

2. What management information is available and regularly used for control of the business?

Question: why does the business have any kind of structure to it at all? Answer: because there are too many activities going on for one person to handle them all. However much you yearn for your former days in the market square and however bad you are at delegating, if you employ staff you're not doing it all yourself. And if you're using other people to do some of it you can't keep track of everything yourself. *Ergo*, you must have an information system, some process by which you ensure that the right information gets to the appropriate people (yourself included) so that they know what they need to know in order to take informed decisions. Now you know what it is, but is the one you've got good enough?

There are two constant sources of amazement in this context — that some businessmen try to run their businesses with so little information because they have no system, and that others who do have a system don't get the right control data from it or use it constructively (more of this in Chapter 4). For present purposes you should try to establish two things: what information (if any) is generated within the business for control purposes and what use is made of it. Answering these questions may be a time-consuming matter (delegate it to the finance director!) but quite frankly, there is little point in establishing a corporate strategy without a decent system to monitor your progress. So start now by defining the system as it is and establishing its value.

The information that we're considering here covers such items as (on a monthly basis) sales by product, cost of items sold, monthly overhead, profit(!), debtor balances, creditor balances,

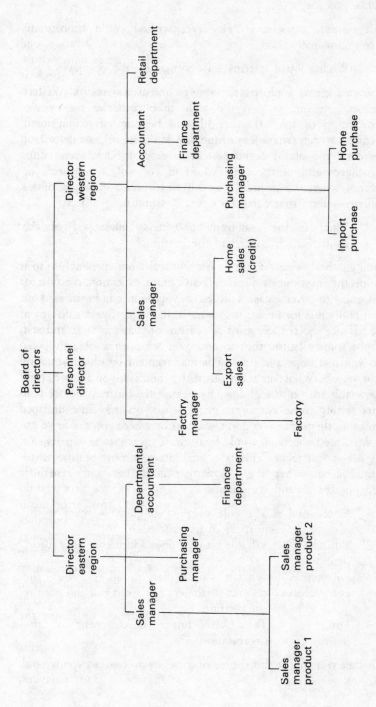

Figure 1. *Company organisation chart*

unit output, stock levels etc (ever wished you'd become an accountant instead?).

3.   What control systems exist to manage the business?

You can get as sophisticated about control systems as you feel inclined. At one end of the scale they comprise merely the expectation of the MD that he will be handed management accounts within two weeks of the end of the month. At the other, we're talking about a full system of responsibility accounting. Whichever end of the scale you find yourself, the process of defining where the business is now must include a statement of the control systems that currently operate within it.

4.   What is the management/business philosophy of the controllers or owners of the business?

Finally, then, one of the most difficult but probably most important questions of this indulgence in introspection. Answering it is going to cover areas as diverse as why you're in business at all (is it really just for profit? if so what's that expensive car doing on the balance sheet? there must be reasons of status as well, and just maybe some altruism too) to how you achieve the objectives set (do you just hope and pray or is management by objective more your style?). Whatever turns out to be the case, you must have a reasonable idea of the philosophy behind the business before you start setting those corporate goals – or you may just find on achieving them that you don't want to be where you are at all. A sophisticated approach would be to draw up what the experts call a mission statement. This is a qualitative, almost philosophical definition of what the company stands for and generally incorporates the following items:

1.	Contextual	The role of this company – what is the purpose of its existence?
2.	Business definition	What it actually does and who it does it for.
3.	Distinctive competences	What it is particularly good at doing – the reasons customers buy from you and not the competition.
4.	Future indicators	The likely future development of the organisation.

Whether you choose this degree of detail or not, unless you have a clear idea of the philosophy of the business you cannot design a future that will fit.

Personnel-related

Now you know something about your context, you've got some broad parameters on where you are financially, and you have a few ideas on what's right and wrong with your internal structure. But just when you thought it was safe to go back into the water some bright spark mentions personnel. For the enlightened, it's fashionable to talk about staff as the most important asset of the business. Close, but not close enough: the number one asset of your business is your customer list. Forget that, let anything else usurp the throne in your thinking and you can pack your corporate bags and go home. But – and it's a big but – staff are indeed your second most important asset. Treat them right and they'll go the second mile time after time. Treat them wrong for too long and they'll vote with their feet. So one way or another your people must have a prominent place in your corporate plan. Reference has already been made to the need to involve key staff in the drafting of the plan and the establishment of targets they will have responsibility for achieving, but go further than that:

1. Which staff are functioning at the height of their ability and which have further potential that you have yet to exploit?

Working quietly away in businesses across the land are people who in years to come will launch out on their own, become successful and perhaps make millions into the bargain. Behind every successful ex-employee stands his bewildered and bemused ex-employer. If you've got someone like that in your organisation, do whatever you can to keep him or her. That way at least some of his talent will create success in your business. But perhaps the problem is not so much one of keeping talented employees happy, rather it's a question of recognising their ability in the first place. If your business is to become more successful than it is now you must recognise and retain talent. To do so you must start to identify it now. If the organisation is too big for you to be familiar with everyone in it, train your managers to recognise talent and not stifle it because they see it as a threat.

2. How many employees does the business have and in which

area of the business do they function?
3.   What is the ratio of management to staff?

If you can't answer question 2 reasonably accurately on the spot then take one black mark. Find out, and add numbers to the organisational chart. As far as question 3 is concerned, have you ever sat down and thought scientifically about optimum management/staff ratios? How many operational staff can a manager oversee and still be in control? The answer depends on both the nature of the activity and the style of management adopted. Suffice to say that if you don't know, now's the time to start thinking about it.

4.   What rewards and incentives are offered and why?

Employee incentive schemes are as numerous in style as there are managers and management consultants to think them up. But good old inertia tends to take its toll here and reward schemes tend to stay in place as if bolted to the floor. The classic example is a firm of builders in south London who had always paid site labour a bonus without thinking about it. When the recession came they just went right on paying, and as wages in the rest of the industry fell, this company's devoted site labour were not only being paid bonuses, but were also getting basic wages of well over the market rate. It was fine until this misplaced generosity almost dragged the company under. The key to avoiding the problem is to define the various components of the remuneration system and then question what objective each is trying to fulfil. Searching, isn't it?

5.   Are employees committed to the success of the company?

It's easy for the outsider to tell the difference between a company with committed employees and one where everyone's a nine-to-fiver. The trouble is, it takes longer to understand the distinction when you're on the inside. It can also be a major struggle to put it right if it's a problem. Do not underestimate the issue. If you do not have the commitment of your employees your company is unlikely ever to be a major success. Business is teamwork and teams with one member don't fare well on the field. To some managers, motivation comes naturally. To some employees commitment amounts to the size of the wage packet at the end of the week. To others, pay is incidental and commitment a personal issue. To the small, growing company, staff commitment is not an added luxury – it is a fundamental essential. For the purposes of the present exercise, let the strategy team determine the level of commitment that they believe staff currently have to the company. Doing something to improve it is an important enough issue to leave discussing until later.

6. Do you communicate with your staff?

Machines are wonderful things. Given sensible treatment, servicing at regular intervals and enough oil they clatter away happily for years with a minimum of attention. Some managers believe that the same manufacturer's handbook that they bought with the machine can be applied to their staff. Unfortunately, or otherwise, people need attention. OK, so most of them work because they need the money, but they also need much more from their jobs, and understanding those needs and fulfilling them will allow you to get maximum performance from your staff. The right attention will also help get you that coveted commitment mentioned above.

Next time you walk through the office or across the factory floor look at some of the employees, and ask yourself when it was that you last stopped to talk to them. *If there are 50 employees or under in a single location in your organisation you should be speaking to them all every day.* If there are substantially more than 50 the management team should be organised so that someone very senior (preferably on the board) talks to each one every day. If the point isn't already obvious, let it be stated – people like to be talked to (and that doesn't mean talked at); they like to feel they matter. There is nothing that motivates more than praise, and praise costs so little. It is a common travesty of justice in business life that most people get kicked for getting it wrong, but when it comes to getting it right the pat on the back is not nearly so easily forthcoming. Tell the guy he's doing a bad job and you risk demotivating him. Tell him you're pleased with his efforts and suggest ways he could do even better and you engender his commitment. The point is so obviously a truism when put in black and white that it's hard to believe that anyone could disagree. Yet daily across the country managers consistently fail to use this fundamental psychological principle to good effect.

Product-related

It is an interesting comment on respective national psychologies that if you ask a US company director what he does, he'll say he is in fast food (or printing or steel or whatever) whereas the British director asked the same question will usually describe himself as a director. However you describe yourself, however you care to think of your function in life, your job is to produce the goods or services that your company offers and thereby satisfy the requirements of your customers. If your business is to continue being a success and become increasingly so, your corporate plan must lay heavy emphasis on the goods that you produce to sell in the market-place. You need to take a long hard look at those products and ask whether they're the right ones to take you forward for the next five years. In the next stage of the planning process you will set growth targets to take you year by year to a stated goal. Are the products you currently have available going to be bought in sufficient quantities to take you to that goal? A number of general questions therefore arise at this stage:

1. Does the company produce a single or overwhelmingly dominant product?

Most people set up in business on the strength of a single good idea. Unfortunately, in most cases, one-product companies are not good news. When the market is happy to take that product or the need is clearly there for it, you wonder what all the fuss is about. However, when the wind changes direction you start to realise how exposed the one-product company really is. There is nothing to fall back on, nothing to switch production to, nothing to absorb that expensive labour force. It needn't just be a change in the market-place that exposes you. Suppose someone else finds a better, cheaper way of fulfilling the need which your one product addresses? Again, you have nowhere to turn when demand for your output evaporates or indeed, if a change in legislation destroys your market.

In 1983 a small Yorkshire-based stationery company was nearly put out of business through over-dependence on a single product. It had achieved considerable success in the sale of scented erasers which had become popular with children at the time. Sadly, one or two small children choked to death as a result of trying to swallow them. A television publicity campaign resulted in a very swift change in legislation and virtually overnight the product was banned from sale in the UK. Fortunately for the company, it was able to dispose of the product abroad, albeit at a loss, and the business was preserved. The rights and wrongs of whether the product should have been sold at all are not at issue here, but the example does serve to illustrate the dangers generally of concentrating too heavily on too few products. The obvious solution to the problem is to diversify, by one route or another. (More of this in Chapter 7.)

2. Where in their life cycle are your present products now?

Product life cycles are highly variable things. At one extreme are the old diehards like matches, which seem to go on virtually forever on a gradually downward sloping path and at the other, high technology items (such as digital watches) whose life is much shorter. Figure 2 illustrates graphically the two extremes. It is essential to get a feel for both the type of life cycle your products follow and where in the cycle they are now. Clearly, there are times when you won't be able to predict the future with any

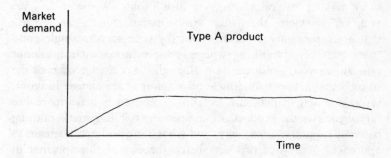

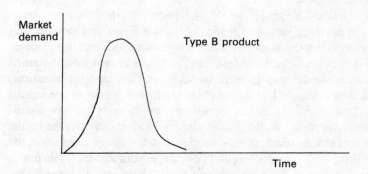

Figure 2. *Product life cycles*

degree of accuracy and even a type A product can face dramatic changes in market requirement. However, if you're in type B markets and the chances are that the life cycles of your products will be relatively short, you need to plan both production and product development with the utmost care. Too many companies find themselves with stocks of type B products that either the market does not want or will not buy at a price that covers their bought-in or production cost.

3. Are products individually evaluated for profitability?

Can you put your hand on your heart and say that you know the true contribution or gross profit of every product or contract that you handle? If the answer is no, then you're driving in the dark without headlights. You do not know which of your products are contributing to the profitability of your company. If you have a profitability problem you do not know which products are causing it by making no contribution towards profits. Worse still, have you ever considered that you might be manufacturing loss-makers that are eating into the profits made by your successful lines?

As part of establishing where you are now, you must look critically at your products from all angles. Are they good enough to fulfil the market requirement at which they are aimed? In what respects are they deficient and how could such deficiencies be remedied? Are the products of competitors fulfilling market needs better than yours? If so, why, and what can you learn from their approach? Will your products reach the end of their profitable lives within the foreseeable future? What plans should be developed for the phased introduction of replacements?

Developmental
Take heart! The process of establishing where the business is now is approaching its grand finale. In the whole process of planning the future of the business, don't forget to include the department whose business really is planning – research and development. Most small companies seem to take the view that they are too small to research. Unfortunately, this attitude is part of the hand-to-mouth, chasing-the-tail syndrome to which so many small businesses succumb. If it hasn't already become clear, let the point be made that planning is a continuous process. It does not end with the production of your five-year corporate plan. That plan, once drafted, will be revised and updated as time passes to take account of development in all factors that influence the business.

Conclusion? There must be somebody or bodies in your organisation responsible for product development. Even if you're not big enough for a department, even if you have no need for full-scale technical development, research and development must become an integral part of your business:

1. Whose responsibility is it to research market trends?
2. Who evaluates products regularly to gauge life cycle developments?
3. Who keeps track of new products that you may wish to bring on stream?
4. Who takes regular critical looks at your existing product range to see if it is suffiiciently comprehensive?
5. Who is to be primarily responsible for co-ordinating the implementation of the corporate plan and, in due course, preparing for the next one?

Do you get that old familiar sinking feeling as you read down the list? Most of the requirements point firmly to the MD's chair. And if research and development (in its widest sense) has indeed been neglected in the past, beginning a new corporate plan is as good an opportunity as you will get to let the wind of change blow through the organisation.

Marketing-related
All the areas examined so far are amenable to corporate planning. Marketing has been left until last because it is the very essence of what corporate strategy is all about. Define a corporate strategy without a marketing plan and you have wasted your time. By all means look at other areas of the business first to establish their more obvious defects, but when you come to look at the feasibility of the targets you are setting and how you intend them to be achieved, the whole planning concept has to be marketing-led. Hence, when we come to the second and third stages of the planning process (defining the targets and establishing the route from here to there) the emphasis will be heavily on marketing.

Now, let it be carved in 10-foot stone tablets if necessary, but get one point clear from the start: marketing is not advertising. Marketing is about creating an environment into which you can sell a product profitably. It is, therefore, about the product itself, the price at which it is sold, the market-place to which it is addressed and only last of all about promotion, of which one aspect may be advertising. If boards of directors understood this relatively simple matter and its importance to their business, it is highly likely that we could have a much stronger competitive industrial base in this country.

However, to bring the point down to earth and for the purpose of looking at where the business is now, you need to take as long and hard a look at your marketing activities as any other area of the business. It's time to sit down with the marketing director again to ask some searching questions. Reference was made earlier to the contextual considerations that need to be borne in mind when defining the company's existing position. However, having established just what market it is that you are in and where you place yourself in it, try considering matters that relate to your activities and your products within that market. For example, try the following:

1. How is the company distinguished from its competitors in the market-place?

Even if your business is totally without repeat sales (and there are very few that are in reality) you depend to some degree on reputation. Ask yourself the question 'for what are we known in our market?' Quality? Timeliness? Efficiency? Price? Breakdowns? Inefficiency? Rudeness? No product is ever sold exclusively on its ability to carry out its design function. There is always an additional element of buying from A rather than B for a whole host of reasons. Similarly, and contrary to popular opinion, price is rarely the only factor considered by a purchaser. Most buyers would prefer to pay more for an equivalent product if by doing so they were confident of delivery times, reliability or even simply because A is more pleasant to do business with than B. Establish what it is that you are known for in the market. If it's nothing in particular, establish which positive reputational factors would be likely to have the greatest impact and go for those. If the market is worried about delivery dates, establish a reputation for timely delivery. Sell the concept to your sales people (they're the ones who have to sell it to the customer) and push it as part of the image in your next advertising campaign. Corporate image is of fundamental significance in business and yet must be one of the most under-used marketing tools known to man.

2. How are products themselves marketed, both existing and new?

Marketing strategies are of necessity as varied as the products they are intended to promote. You cannot market fashion clothes in the same manner as you do conveyancing services, nor turnkey engineering installations in the same way as canned peas. It is not the function of this text to tell you how to market – good advice is available elsewhere on the subject. However, there are some fundamental ground rules that apply to all products and services and for the purposes of establishing your current approach, try considering them.

(a) How do you ensure customers feel they are doing the right thing by buying from you?

(b) How good are you at matching the customer's wants with your ability to meet those wants?

(c) How good are you at honestly admitting your inability to satisfy a want when you are truly unable to do so?

(d) Do you avoid knocking the competition?

(e) What can you learn from your competitors' strategies in all the above, and how can you distinguish your approach from theirs in a way relevant to your customers?

(f) How often do you look at your company and its products from the customer's point of view?

3. Are you innovative in your marketing?

The key to growth lies in the ability to adapt. The world is a changing place, and those that die the lingering corporate death are the ones that will not change with it. But even if your product base is changing and though your production and management systems are state-of-the-art, do you resist change in marketing strategy? If you are the kind of MD who will put this book down having finished it and do nothing practical as a result, you should worry about your willingness to be innovative.

4. Is the company marketing-led?

We all know that the company that does not sell profitably is dead. Unfortunately there are those (very often the ones run by production or research oriented people) who regard sales as the necessary evil that allows production or product design to take place. Such companies may and often do survive but they will never be as profitable as if they started the cycle by asking first what the market needs and then meeting those needs. Reference was made earlier to a confectionery manufacturer with an organisational deficiency. The same company also had a marketing problem (and it just happened to be run by a technical MD) along the lines described above. Customers were necessary evils, the product was king. It was an immense tribute to the product that it had sold so well for so long without any serious marketing. When the new owners got their feet under the table and locked the former MD (who actually stayed after the transfer of ownership) in the development room, one of the first exercises they undertook was the development of a comprehensive marketing plan. The change in orientation came as a great relief to the customers and also contributed substantially to the change in the company's fortunes.

Inevitably, the above gives only an indication of the kinds of question that you should be asking about your existing marketing activities. There will be a long list of others that arise because you and your marketing director know your market best – and if you don't you've identified one of your most significant problems anyway. And if the point has not been made clearly enough already, let it be spelled out here: the marketing process and your consideration of what you do by way of marketing has to be undertaken in the clear light of what the competition is up to. In fact, there is a case for saying that you should analyse the competitors' marketing and promotional activity in much the same manner and depth as you do your own to ensure the foundation is properly laid for policy decisions that are soon to be made.

Summary

The most important intention of this chapter has been to make you *think* about your business as it is now, its deficiencies and problems, potential and possibilities. To do the job properly may be painful at times but if you commit yourself to the task you will have achieved the philosopher's goal – to know himself. Some of the issues raised here have been dealt with at length, so it may help to summarise the logic and principal steps before going any further.

To get the most out of establishing where you are now, follow a few simple but tried and tested rules:

- Get started now or you'll never get started at all.

- Involve key staff.
- Commit everything important to paper.
- Don't let the planning exercise become an excuse for failing to act now.

Adopt a categorised approach to establishing where your business is now. Adopt any categories that suit the business but make sure you cover the following areas somewhere:

- Financial
- Contextual
- Internal
- Personnel
- Product
- Development
- Marketing

Do not necessarily follow the categories slavishly but make sure that somewhere you provide the answers to the questions raised earlier in this chapter.

When the process is finished, if all concerned have done a proper job, you should have as detailed and frank a dossier on the current state of your business as you are ever likely to get. Because it is not human nature to pose questions without raising potential answers, you may also be part way to achieving the next stages of the process by defining targets and routes for achieving them. If so, you'll be ready to move on to the next stages of the process as developed in Chapters 3 and 4. But by now you may also have developed one intangible benefit sought in vain by many groups of diverse individuals in business – the ability to work as a team and to respect and respond to the opinions of others.

Chapter 3
Ending at the Right Destination

So now you're sitting at your desk, dossier on the company's present status in front of you, feeling pretty satisfied with your achievements. You know more about the organism that constitutes your company than you ever did before. Its strengths, weaknesses, opportunities and potential are all laid out before you. There's been some blood-letting but to see the way that the board has functioned as a team it's all been worthwhile. However, before you get too self-satisfied and smug, spare a thought for why you indulged in this orgy of introspection in the first place. Remember, you agreed that there is very little success that isn't planned; that you decided that the only way to get the business to go somewhere, to fulfil its real potential, was to develop a full corporate strategy. And oh yes, the process of defining where the business is now was only stage one in that process. Before you give up in despair at the thought of yet more soul searching, bear in mind that you have actually completed the most demanding stage of the process; the rest is largely a matter of logical thought and management skills. The best place to start stage two therefore is with a question:

Why were we here in the first place?

Answer: you were here in the first place in order to develop a long-term plan for the future of the company, set targets that you want to achieve in the future and decide on the best strategy for getting from A to B. Now, as a result of all those questions you asked yourself and your board in Chapter 2, some of the aims for the future are going to drop into place quite naturally. If you have identified clear areas of weakness, if you have defined obvious constraints on your ability to grow, remedial action for such deficiencies is a must, whatever your global corporate goals turn out to be. Follow the same rules of the road set out in Chapter 2 – involve other people, write down your conclusions and so on. But before you get too excited about specifics, remember that the aim of this stage of the planning process is to establish comprehensive co-ordinated goals for the business as a whole (strategic goals) within which you can develop shorter-term goals for each segment of the business (tactical goals). So don't start by letting the production director rush off to double plant capacity simply because he foresees bottlenecks – at least not until the marketing and finance directors have between them established that the saleable and organisationally feasible level of production will induce such bottlenecks given present capacity.

The setting of most co-ordinated targets will, in fact, be likely to start with financial figures at the sales end. You may wish to start by aiming at, say, trebling your turnover over the next five years, and raising net profitability on turnover from X to Y per cent. Before going any further, consider deeply the implications of what you are saying. What market share will such an increase give you? Indeed, is the market growing at such a rate that you could achieve that target without increasing market share at all? What will be the response of the competition to your aggressive expansionist policy? Which means are feasible to enhance net profit percentage? Will it be done by price rises? Cost of sales reductions? Overhead reduction?

At this stage you do not have to establish definitively the strategy for achieving your goals, only that those goals are feasible in the light of the practical action that can be taken to enhance the business – not like the inventor of an improved engineering process who went to the trouble and cost of designing a business plan on the strength of his invention, assembling the necessary management team and so on, only to find that on approaching venture capitalists for funding (on the strength of figures he himself supplied) he needed some 10 per cent of the world market just to break even!

If you start with the establishment of global financial objectives (turnover, profitability and cash generation) many of the non-financial targets follow logically. To get the sort of turnover increases you're seeking you must get your marketing sewn up or you'll find yourself breaking the cardinal rule and cutting price merely to increase turnover volume. Market share and ranking targets will follow naturally from your turnover aim and market growth estimates. If there is instability in the market you will need to set targets with regard to stabilising it (if it is responsive to your influence) or diversifying into more stable environments. If you already have potential sourcing difficulties the quickest way to bring them to a head is to demand substantially increased output from your suppliers. You need to establish a policy for releasing the constraint before it becomes a problem. If you're not adequately structured the chances of successfully achieving your defined goals will be seriously diminished. Similarly, if your information systems are inadequate you will not be able to monitor progress or rectify deviations from budget.

And so the list goes on. In fact, in most of the questions specified in Chapter 2, establishing primary financial targets will result in strong pointers towards the goals you must set for each segment of the business. It is possible, however, to start the process by specifying non-financial targets as your primary goals – possible but dangerous. There may be an intrinsic attraction in aiming at 10 per cent of the home market and 50 per cent of turnover being exported within five years, but the summary financial implication must be clearly specified to assess the feasibility of the aim. Returning to the Welsh crafting company mentioned in Chapter 2, another mistake made by the autocratic chief executive lay in this area. He set a target of being the biggest producer in his generic category within five years. But not only did he fail to enlist support in setting such targets, he also failed to understand that to achieve the goal would set impossible turnover targets for a number of his divisions. The result was that managers cut price to achieve the targets, and profitability in those divisions plummeted. Food for thought, isn't it?

For most companies, the best place to start is with the setting of summary financial targets, but short of pulling figures out of the air, how do you establish initially what is an acceptably ambitious aim? Consideration needs to be given to the psychological and motivational aspects of goal setting (see below) but in answering the question think about the following:

1. What rate of growth and profitability have comparable companies historically been able to achieve? All things being equal, set your sights a little higher than their achievements.
2. What level of growth would allow you just to keep pace with market growth? Unless market share is unimportant,

aim to set targets above market growth rates.

3. What increased pressures will a given growth rate exert on your working capital requirements? *On no account allow yourself to overtrade unless you have immediate access to additional sources of working capital.* (Overtrading is defined as growing at a rate that demands more working capital, eg stocks, debtors etc than your profit can supply.)

The matter of working capital, cash availability and trading levels bears closer inspection. Most new businessmen setting out are grateful to take any trade that comes their way for obvious reasons. When it comes to planning the future the temptation is to take precisely the same approach. However, before committing yourself, just sit back and consider the implications of the growth targets that you are about to adopt.

1. For an extra £1,000 sale on 1 June, a raw material purchase of £250 on 1 March which has to be paid for on 1 April.
2. Direct labour to work on the product for three months, say £150 per month between March and May – that's another £450.
3. At the end of May, delivery costs, say another £50.
4. If you're quick and get the invoice out in the first week of June you may be lucky enough to get paid by 1 August.

Here's the problem: between 1 April and 1 August you're carrying increased costs of between £250 and £750 and that's without taking into account the increased warehousing, overheads etc that you can reasonably expect when you're on a growth path. Multiply it by 100 and the numbers are big. If you have the capital base to finance the requirement yourself, or the assets to secure a loan from your friendly neighbourhood bank manager, fine. If not, you're in trouble. You'll be short of liquid funds all the time, delaying one creditor to pay another and generally ruining customer goodwill in an attempt to get them to pay more quickly. Ultimately, if you do it on a grand enough scale, someone's going to put you out of business because he's tired of waiting to be paid. Overtrading isn't worth the trouble it causes. Either establish a growth path that you can manage out of existing cash resources and be grown up enough to turn away business you cannot finance for the time being or arrange for the finance to be available, although admittedly that's easier said than done.

Two contrasting examples will serve to emphasise the point. Brendon Enterprises Limited was a company in the north-east running a restaurant chain under the control of an energetic entrepreneur. The restaurants were theme-based and potentially very successful. The problem was that the owner couldn't wait for the first to be properly established and trading profitably before opening the second. This took much longer to get off the ground than anticipated, and threatened for a while to drag both down. Long before the second was properly established the third was under construction. Each time Peter, the ordinary creditor (and inevitably the Inland Revenue) was robbed to finance Paul, the new venture. Inevitably, time finally ran out and the really big cash crisis arose. Extremely large sums had to be expended on expensive accountants (who in such circumstances nearly always want their fees up front). It emerged that the only way to save the business was to sell half of it (for much less than it was really worth) to an outsider who had the resources to bail it out. The third project was cancelled, and the growth rate moderated. Of course, if the entrepreneur had bitten the bullet and done just the same six months earlier he could have ended up holding on to the whole company.

By contrast, the bathroom accessories manufacturers mentioned on page 10 adopted a wholly different approach. All their strategic decisions were taken in consideration of the resources available to the company. Only on one occasion did they become over-exposed, and that through the unpredictable movements in the market rather than unwise action on their own part. However, the directors called in management consultants to look at the growth rate of the company in its latter stages as a private company. While turnover had been growing at a relatively consistent figure per annum, the percentage growth rate year by year had been declining. The decision was taken to stabilise the growth rate in percentage terms, if possible at 25 per cent per annum. A detailed examination of the working capital required to sustain this rate indicated that funds might well become short in due course. It was partly in the light of this information that the directors decided to bring the company on to the stock market. A flotation was arranged and the business was successfully provided with the finance it needed for expansion.

The point should be fairly clear by now; in summary, the crucial features of the long-term plan that you are establishing now are the turnover and profit targets that you are setting yourself, and the growth rates that they imply, together with the cash implications of those targets.

If you are going to the trouble of establishing a corporate strategy, go to the trouble of setting the right growth targets. Most corporate plans will, in essence, be plans for achieving a stated financial target. That target is itself the corner-stone – get it right and the rest should follow. Get it wrong and the plan will be meaningless and everybody's efforts in trying to achieve it will be not only wasted but harmful and demoralising as well.

Non-financial goals

All this emphasis on financial aspects, while totally valid, is in danger of making you forget about the other features of the business examined in Chapter 2. As far as contextual considerations are concerned, as mentioned earlier, such features as ranking and market share tend to follow naturally from financial targets and if sourcing is a problem, now is the time to sort it out. But the examination of the company's context should have raised some rather more fundamental questions on matters such as market stability and adequacy of premises. Once again, now is the time to be taking decisions on whether your present market offers the room for growth that you are looking for or whether it's time to be establishing new means of expansion. The long cold look that you should have taken at the existing market may have led to some inevitable implications – like the only way to survive is to get out by some means or other. If so, set the targets for doing so within the range of objectives that you are now establishing.

Organisational structure is an area which seems duty bound to give most MDs sleepless nights. The problem is that if a structure hasn't been designed, it will have come about through custom and practice. Woe betide the ambitious manager who tries to redraw the boundaries once the pecking order has been established informally. But if your examination forces the conclusion that the structure of your organisation is inadequate, change must come, however painful. However, a word of warning is appropriate. Do not try to change the organisation too fast. Businesses are made up of people and people are concerned about status and job security. Protect your second most important asset and it will jump through hoops for you; upset it and resentment will grow like a cancer. For now, confine yourself to defining on paper the structure of organisation (together with names and reporting channels) that would be optimal for the business that you want to be by the end of the planning period. You can worry later how you're going to get there without losing your key staff.

Similarly, an adequate information system is a must for you to be able to monitor progress towards stated goals. Defining and installing a system that will generate adequate control information may well be a job for which you have to call on professional help. But establishing the strategy for getting to the targets will include setting budgets (probably annual, subdivided monthly) as stepping stones towards those targets. Without a competent information system you will be unable to monitor progress.

When it comes to people, planning over an extended period can be much more difficult, simply because it is difficult to be confident which members of staff are likely to be working for the organisation at the end of that period. If you can identify key individuals whose loss would be particularly damaging to the organisation, the only solution is to make it worth their while to stay on a long-term basis. Their current remuneration and prospects for advancement have to be sufficient to make them stay put. One widely used device that can be very effective is to let such individuals acquire an interest in the business through share options schemes. But however it's done, plan a means for key people to be kept in place for the foreseeable future. Fail to plan adequately and the outcome will be the same as any other aspect of the business that has been improperly planned – not what you would like.

As far as the rest of the workforce is concerned, plan for it as a single body. If the management to staff ratio is wrong, plan to get it right as soon as possible. If the staff turnover rate is high, by now you should have a fair idea of why. Plan to put the deficiencies right, and plan to have it done by a specified date – vague intentions of 'as soon as possible' will not stop the rot. And as far as communication with the workforce is concerned you don't even have to plan; it's a case of doing it now. Talk to your staff formally and informally. Set clear lines of official communication and run an open-door policy at the same time. Out there on the factory floor and even in the typing pool is a bottomless well of ideas on how to do the job better, ideas that come from the people that do the jobs every day of their working lives. Use that asset – it's freely available.

In Chapter 2, having covered the aspects of the business examined above, attention was turned to products, research and marketing. The only summary goal it is possible to adopt for each of these areas is that they should be sufficiently well developed to support the targets set for growth and stability. Products, product innovation and marketing strategy are tools for the achievement of targets. Development plans must be formulated for each, but in the light of the goals set for the business as a whole. Consequently, once the overall corporate plan has been determined, it will be necessary to work the implications through into a marketing plan, a development plan and a production and business plan. Planning in these areas, particularly marketing, is likely to result in positive action for the achievement of targets outside the general categories themselves, eg the goal of marketing is to sell product and achieve turnover. The goal of a production and innovation strategy is to have demanded product on the market in order to allow sales to be made to achieve the turnover targets.

All this is in danger of becoming a little esoteric. In summary, the point is this: establish overall goals, preferably financial targets that you feel can be achieved by the end of the planning period. Next, set out sub-targets for the various divisions of the organisation, some of which follow naturally from the financial targets, others of which will have to be determined by policy. Subsequent chapters will delve into the subject of establishing marketing and other strategies for the achievement of determined goals.

The psychology of target setting

Reference was made above to financial targets that you feel can be *achieved by the end of the planning period*.

As yet, no direct reference has been made in this chapter to the period which the full corporate plan should cover. Inevitably, there is no definitive answer since the optimum period is likely to be specific to the individual business. Therefore, when deciding on the period over which you will plan, take account not only of the problems that you have identified in stage one, but also the cycles that your industry experiences, and the stage at which your principal products are in their own cycles. It is difficult to see how any plan covering less than three years could be described as strategic. Most plans will probably be based on a five-year horizon, largely because in most industries it is difficult to see any further ahead with an acceptable degree of accuracy. However, in some cases, the period may be much longer, especially in an industry with long predictable cycles. Take A P Green & Co Limited which, in the early 1970s, was a small family building business based in Surrey. The company had operated for a number of years building no more than half-a-dozen houses per year.

The proprietor decided over a period of months that he had had enough of getting his boots dirty on site, and that the only way for him to become a manager rather than an operative was for the business to grow. As the building industry functions on very long cycles (anything up to 18 years according to some experts), he was able to plan far ahead with reasonable confidence in how the industry would perform for many years to come. In addition, he was producing a product where demand was assured. Sure enough he cranked the handle and over a ten-year period ended up with the large local building firm he had been aiming at, and did it without overtrading, and in an industry notorious for its crashes and cowboys. However, for us lesser mortals, five years is likely to be the limit, although as already discussed, on a rolling basis.

The psychology of target setting does not stop with getting the time horizon right. It's easy when taking an overview of matters to gloss over problems, but just stop and think for a moment about what the target setting is going to involve. Someone, in full consideration of the relevant facts, figures and estimates is going to set specific goals for the whole of the firm and each of its constituent parts, to which they will commit themselves totally for a long time to come. Who should do that target setting and just how ambitious should the goals be? The obvious answer to the first question is that your (by now) tried and trusted board of directors should be charged with the task. But once those targets are set, whose responsibility is it going to be to achieve them and the budgets that stage the way to their achievement? In overall terms, it probably will be the board, but what about the individual managers at sub-board level? In short, who is actually responsible for managing the achievement of those targets or any part of them and who gets kicked for any failure to hit budget? The psychology of target setting amounts to this: you cannot hold any person responsible for the achievement of a budget unless he has had a hand in setting that budget. In addition, you cannot be sure that the budget is feasible unless the individuals responsible for its achievement have participated in its establishment. So, everyone involved in managing the achievement of the budget must participate in its establishment.

The question now arises, to what extent can you substitute 'strategic target' for 'budget' in the argument above? Middle managers, or so the theory goes, are tactical thinkers, capable of absorbing the concept of a one-year budget but no more. It takes the strategic thinkers in the board room to conceive of a five-year time horizon. There is an element of truth in this approach. You cannot expect the man whose nose is always to the grindstone suddenly to sit back and think without warning about the next five years. But where the whole idea of corporate planning started was with the idea that even your board needed to think more strategically and, hopefully, by now they've adjusted to it. In addition, if you don't involve your managers, how do you hold them responsible for each annual budget that marks the way to the five-year goal? Each of those annual budgets will, in total, follow logically from the strategic plan. The conclusion must, by now, be obvious. Those responsible for achievement of any target must have an input into the plan.

Nor does the psychology stop there. The means by which managers (and for that matter, the board) have that input may be crucial for the chances of achieving maximum sustainable growth over the period. It is not sufficient to ask Fred how much turnover (and cost) he's going to do this year and put the relevant figures in as Fred's input. Start from the other end. Where do you want the company to be in five years? Take the answer and break it down into annual growth targets and then analyse the implications for Fred. Do you think he's capable of doing what's implied? Is he capable of doing more or less? Propose a growth target to him and allow a margin for negotiation. Ideally, the final figure should be just attainable with maximum reasonable effort. Finalise it at too low a level and you're unlikely to get the best out of Fred. Set it too high and one of two things will happen: either Fred will become disheartened at the impossible job which has been set him and give up even trying to achieve target or he will go all out to hit it this year (and possibly achieve it) but he'll be so exhausted that there is no chance of hitting next year's target. Somewhere in this world of compromise lies the balance between obtaining the most mileage possible out of a situation and not ruining your chances by being over-ambitious. To state the obvious, you're all going to have to live with a rolling five-year plan for ever. Before your finalise it, make sure it is acceptable to all who will be measured by it.

There is one further aspect of target setting worthy of

consideration from the viewpoint of the amateur psychologist, that which the experts call 'goal congruence'. This has been touched on to some extent in the previous chapter and in fact, the manager commitment to growth targets mentioned above is part of it. The essence of the concept is that you get much more from an employee if he is personally committed to what you are trying to make him achieve than if his only incentive in life is the monthly pay cheque. As far as its relevance to planning is concerned, you can aim at goal congruence in two contexts: general employee commitment to the company itself and specific commitment to the plan.

For some unfortunate and incomprehensible reason, goal congruence is widely perceived as an Americanism with little relevance to UK businesses. It is certainly true that the psychological approach is more prevalent in the US environment than in Merrie England, but that is to their benefit and our shame. The value of it is there for all to see in the performance statistics of those companies which are most conscious of it. Anglicise it by calling it 'employee loyalty' and its value becomes obvious. When stripped of jargon and technique, goal congruence amounts to treating employees right, giving them what they want and making them feel worthwhile. If this is beginning to sound repetitive, it's because it is one of the most important lessons for any business to learn. Having arrived at the enviable state of goal congruence in the company itself, that same commitment can be usefully employed in serving the aims of the corporate plan. Do not be secretive about the plan. Let employees be aware that the company is working on a strategy and that they are the only ones who will make it work. You do not need to go into graphic detail but it can be worth trying to explain in ways that they will understand: it is amazing how much better people feel, how much more they identify with an organisation simply because they are told what is going on.

Measuring achievement

The corporate planning process is now well under way. You have established a clear understanding of where you are starting from and you now know what your objectives are. In addition, you are ready to translate a five-year target into annual budgets. But before you go any further, how do you intend to measure achievement of your goals and assess the benefits of the planning process in which you have engaged? Measurement is crucial to the process but simply to compare budget with actual achievement is too simplistic an approach, especially for the non-financial aspects of the plan. The only means of monitoring progress that is likely to succeed is to assign overall responsibility for all objectives contained in the plan and to hold regular meetings of all those responsible to review that progress. No form of written assessment is a substitute for face-to-face discussion in this context. The requirement is time-consuming but worthwhile if the process is to be effective. In addition, bear in mind that however firm your intentions now, some of the targets in the plan are likely to be modified in the light of changing circumstances. If monitoring is exclusively on a written or numerical basis there is a greater tendency to follow initial objectives slavishly. Treat the plan the same as any other board level matter in this context. Talk about it, develop it, modify it if necessary. But review progress face to face, frequently and regularly. In an environment where matters are addressed in order of urgency, long-term strategic issues tend to go to the bottom of everyone's pile. Make them the exclusive subject of a special meeting and, magically, they assume a greater priority in everyone's thinking.

Summary

The principal intention of this chapter has been to examine the establishment of targets for the business and each part of it in the context of knowing where you are starting from. The process of establishing goals will normally start with financial parameters such as turnover and net profitability which may imply special targets for some of the non-financial areas in which goals have to be set. In addition, any specific weaknesses or limitations unearthed during the process of defining where the business is now will imply targets for their own resolution. The primary financial targets (turnover and profitability) should be set with a clear eye on what is feasible within the industry, geographic locality and the context of the business itself and it is particularly important to establish growth targets commensurate with the working capital available to the business at any time.

The key to the success of the organisation is the people working for it. Make sure that the best of them stay with you and that all are properly looked after. Be aware of the psychological impact of the targets that you set.

- Establish sensible time scales.
- Involve those responsible for achieving targets in setting them.
- Set goals that are feasible but require effort for achievement.
- Use the planning process to engender workforce commitment.

Finally, measure achievement by holding regular meetings with no other items on the agenda and do not be afraid to modify specified goals in the light of new developments.

Chapter 4
Choosing the Route

You are now effectively two-thirds of the way to establishing a corporate plan, in that you have determined where the company is now and where you can feasibly expect it to be at the end of the planning period, at least with regard to financial targets. In addition, you will have identified those aspects of the business that are weak, or likely to limit your ability to grow. Realistically, because the process cannot be divided into watertight compartments, you will also have begun to give some thought to how you intend to get from where you are now to where you want to be. Most corporate strategies are designed to result in the growth of the company, and growth goals can be set in a variety of ways (to be biggest, to make net profits of £x etc). But essentially, they all come back to the same question: what is the best method of raising turnover and net profitability of the economy without exposing it to undue danger? Certain principles will apply whichever way the question is answered.

1. The company must have an information system capable of generating accurate and timely information for control purposes – no corporate plan will be workable without it.
2. All the company's resources must be used to the fullest extent, including human resources.
3. No attempt must be made to increase turnover at a rate which will leave the company short of working capital (overtrading) unless an injection of additional finance is feasible.
4. If the company is one of a small number of large producers in an industry or locality it must not be assumed that competitors will stand idly by and watch their markets being taken – they will react!

5. The company must not become over-dependent upon one supplier or customer unless it can be absolutely certain that the relationship will not become a problem.

6. It is important not to overestimate the length of the life cycle of a product, particularly in a young industry.

These are fundamentals, the case for which has been argued already, but their importance needs to be emphasised and you have to take full account of them in establishing the strategy.

In summary, there are essentially four categories of action which can be taken to get from A to B. They are far from being mutually exclusive and the case studies which follow will show how some companies have used a number of them at various times during their planning phases. They are:

- growth in turnover of existing activities;
- diversification;
- acquisition;
- internal reorganisation

The following chapters will examine each of these areas in considerable depth, since, in truth, they represent the essence of corporate planning. However, a word of warning is appropriate. Corporate planning is an activity in which the end wholly and exclusively justifies the means. Once you set the strategy, embark upon it and allocate responsibility for its components, it is all too easy to emphasise the means and lose sight of the objectives. Do not let yourself or your employees lose sight of what it is all about. You can have all the fun in the world travelling but in this case, unless you arrive at the right destination or something very like it, you have wasted your time, money and a whole lot of effort. Before going into each of these areas in depth, take a look at the broad parameters which apply to them and see how they were applied by some of those who have travelled this route before.

Growth in turnover of existing activities

There is something intrinsically attractive about simply continuing to do what you have done successfully in the past. The thinking seems to be 'if we have proved successful at widget manufacture to date, we are more likely to be successful at that in the future than at any other activity'. There is obviously a degree of logic in this argument but its application to corporate planning requires two questions to be answered:

1. Can we be confident of sufficient market stability in the future, implying that we need not do anything but grow generically?
2. Are we confident that because we can handle widget manufacture at one level of activity, we shall be able to cope with all the additional problems that jacking up the turnover will bring?

The unspoken assumption that gives rise to this approach to growth is that we have skills in widgets but in no other area. However, contrary to that belief, if you are running a successful company, even if you have been in widgets all your life, you have a second proven area of expertise – that of business management. Many of the managerial skills which you apply to running your own business are equally applicable to a whole host of other activities; management ability is an organisational skill and there are precious few people blessed with an abundance of it (well, judging by that displayed in many companies anyway). The very transferability of that skill means that there is no good reason why you should stick to the generic growth path if other routes offer more advantageous prospects. Indeed, in a potentially unstable industry, forever doing more of the same can have disastrous consequences.

John Brown was a chartered engineer, specialising in large government contracts. When he felt he had picked up enough experience working for someone else, he decided to launch out on his own. Fortuitously, his commencement of trade coincided with the expenditure of their enormous oil wealth by Middle Eastern states. Obviously, a considerable amount of this money was spent on capital projects and John was fortunate enough to pick up a certain amount of this business. In addition, he was doing work tendering for government contracts in the UK. Needless to say, the business grew. Growth was all generic since there was apparently no call for diversification. Government contracts had been placed at a growing rate for as long as John could remember and oil wealth seemed set to have a similar effect on Middle Eastern contracts. The firm expanded, taking on more staff and even establishing its own training programmes. All was well until recession bit. Capital expenditure by the UK government was cut, hitting firms like John's hard. By unfortunate coincidence, the company incurred a number of large bad debts in its overseas operation. Instead of taking the strategic approach which would probably have suggested the need for diversification, the company took defensive action. Conscious of the need to keep turnover up in order to generate work for employees, John's team started reducing quotes on tenders in order to retain market share. Inevitably, the rest of the market took a similar view and reacted the same way. The result was that not only was there less work around to be shared out, but what there was was being undertaken at lower margins. The industry and John's firm along with it had compounded its own problems by failing to take the strategic view. With a reduction in turnover and lower gross margins the effects on net profit (and consequently, cash flow) were easily predictable. The company laid off large numbers of employees, again as a defensive measure. Potentially, with the reduction in costs, the business might have been saved, albeit to operate at a much reduced scale, but in a final blow half of John's management left overnight, unable to cope any longer with his autocratic management style. Ultimately, the company went under, becoming another statistical casualty of the recession. Two lessons are fairly obvious:

1. If the firm had grown by diversification in its earlier days, the impact of recession and bad debts would have been less marked.
2. If John had adopted a less autocratic management style and involved employees more in the running of the company, they would have been more committed and would not have walked out.

There is nothing particularly complicated in these lessons. Indeed, it is perhaps their very simplicity that results in them and others like them being overlooked, but it does tend to undermine the belief that generic growth is the safe way forward. In truth, there is little real safety in business and if you are after the safe, quiet life, question whether you should be in business at all. Nevertheless, while there is little real safety, there are very real means by which risk may be mitigated (the means will vary from case to case) and generic growth is not always the answer.

Diversification

If generic growth is not always the best solution (and indeed may be positively dangerous in some instances), where do you look next for a route to take you to the growth goal? Well, if you don't intend just to do more of the same, you obviously need to diversify (isn't the logic of corporate strategy staggering – your management consultant might charge you thousands for that one). For a detailed examination of the advantages and disadvantages of diversification, together with some ideas on how to do it, see Chapter 7. For now, in the race to avoid the dangers inherent in generic growth, just remember the cardinal rule:

Never allow yourself to lose sight of your existing business which is profitable in the quest of new, diversified, turnover.

The danger, as in most other aspects of this subject, is to lose sight of the wood by concentrating on the trees. There is nothing more interesting than something new. And by now, the idea of corporate planning will have lost some of its glamour (OK, so it never really had any to start with). The danger is that you convince yourself that you are fulfilling the requirements of the strategic approach that you have committed yourself to, while you go off doing (seemingly) much more interesting things like chasing new lines of business. Meanwhile, who is minding the strategic shop? Unfortunately, there are some matters in business which, if the MD doesn't look after, nobody else will – and strategy is one of them. If the decision is that diversification is the best road to go down, then by all means go down it, but always make sure that it is not to the detriment of either the existing business or the strategic approach to which you are now committed.

Take the example of a machine tool manufacturer in the West Midlands conurbation. The company had a long history, having been handed down, father to son, through three generations. As trading became more difficult in the traditional industries during the late 1970s, the company's management turned their attention outward to see what else might be available. Now, one of the problems with a long standing family company is that each generation, being brought up in the business, can come to believe that there is no other business activity worthy of contemplation or, if there is, they do not have the necessary expertise to contemplate it anyway. Indeed, there was an element of such thinking in this case.

So the solution had to lie not simply in a new product but in the acquistion of expert skill in dealing with that product. Yet the company had inadequate funding to acquire a subsidiary. The solution hit upon in this case was merger with another company in a totally different sector of activity whose market functioned on a different cycle. The latter company, of course, had its own reasons for wanting a merger but these were compatible with the machine tool manufacturers. The most interesting feature of the case was that independently, the two companies had lacked strength. Together (though each business was still run separately) they had the muscle to negotiate (particularly with financiers) from a position of strength and obtained better terms. The happy ending to the story came less than 12 months later, when the new group sought and was granted a public quotation, something that neither could have contemplated separately.

Acquisition

As the last case study shows, doing something different need not be a matter of launching out into uncharted territory without a guide. If proper precautions are taken, it can be done successfully with a minimum of risk. Certainly, you would be unwise to engage seriously in any new form of business without buying in expertise, but the way in which you do it need not be restricted to advertising for a new product manager to develop the activity. As an alternative, you can contemplate acquiring the whole of an existing operation.

Growth by acquisition can take one of two forms – either you buy a business doing the same sort of thing as you already do, or one in a totally different field (amazing logic yet again). Bringing to bear that management expertise referred to earlier in the chapter, in time you should be able to run the business better than its previous management. But just a word of warning before you go rushing out to buy a subsidiary; there are two major questions to ask yourself before seriously contemplating a particular acquisition:

1. Does the price justify my buying this business rather than building up my own operation in the same field?
2. Why is the vendor selling? There are many legitimate reasons for selling a business but probably twice as many illegitimate ones. Make very sure that the vendor's true reason for selling is not the reason why you should not be buying.

To take the previous example one stage further, having successfully undertaken their merger, the new joint management decided that they had learned a thing or two about company acquisition along the way and that, given the right circumstances, growth by acquisition could be quite a good idea. In particular, it afforded immediate access to higher levels of profit and turnover. A number of potential targets were identified and eventually they set upon one that fitted the bill most closely. Negotiations were entered into and the proprietors were willing to sell (largely on the grounds of age and lack of management succession). The net result was a group some 30 per cent larger than the acquirer had previously been and a new subsidiary whose activities could be relatively easily integrated into the existing structure – very important from the point of view of not losing sight of the existing business.

By way of interesting comparison, take the example of a small conglomerate that came to public quotation in the mid-1980s. Its top management could have written the set text on corporate strategy and had long since decided that their way forward was by strategic acquisition. Further, they had clearly defined their market and area of expertise. With a few careful exceptions, they grew by acquisition of poorly managed companies within their sector, applying their own proven management techniques to rectify the mistakes of their predecessors. And grow they did! Acquisitions followed one after the other, enough time being allowed between each to resolve major problems, indoctrinate existing management in new methods and identify the next target. The result was a cohesive group, managed by the people that knew best – the experts within each company – and directed strategically from the top by the group board. When it finally decided to come to the market, the reception was rapturous. Much current thinking seems to be along the lines that acquisition, takeover and merger is for the stock market giants. As the above examples illustrate, such need not be the case.

Internal reorganisation

You can grow by doing more of what you already do now and you can grow by starting to do something new, either by diversification or by acquisition. Seemingly, there cannot be any other options. But have you considered the possibility of growing by doing less? Perverse though it may sound, there may actually be some mileage in the idea. Indeed, if you look at what the big boys have been doing (especially the international conglomerates) for the last few years, much of it amounts to exactly this. Many of them have been re-examining their corporate structures, identifying those parts of the group that are either not adequately profitable or do not fit the corporate plan, and disposing of them. The popularity of the management buyout in the mid-1980s has originated largely with this common approach to big business.

Once again, just because it's the big boys who are leading the way doesn't mean that the smaller businesses cannot go the same way if appropriate. However, here it is the words 'if appropriate' that loom large. The interesting thing about disposals of unprofitable businesses is that there is actually somebody who wants to buy them at all. After all, if they are truly non-goers why waste the money? It is very often that the amount of effort and time needed to put them right is more than the parent company can spare. Consequently, they are treated as millstones around the corporate neck, may be disposed of at very low valuations and fall into the lap of local management who are only too eager to take on the 'liability' and very quickly turn it into an asset.

If the truth of the matter is that you really do have loss-making operations which have no serious hope of being turned, then dispose of them and you should see a positive impact on your bottom line profit (leaving aside the question of exception disposal and redundancy costs). But before you take that irreversible decision and sell, take a long, hard look at why there is a problem. Reorganise whatever is necessary to resolve it, wait a while until it is up and running and if you're still determined to dispose of it for other reasons, at least you will then be able to ask a sensible price for what you are selling.

Summary

Assuming that your corporate plan amounts to a blueprint for growth, there are essentially four categories of route for getting from where you are now to where you want to be, any of which can normally be used:

1. Growth in turnover of existing activities; but beware of the dangers of over-concentration on a limited market if you intend to use this, the most obvious route.
2. Diversification; but do not diversity to the detriment of the existing business. Instead, choose diversity that adds to the value of your current operation.
3. Acquisition; not just for the big boys, but make sure the

price is right and the vendor is selling for the right reasons.
4. Internal reorganisation; if there is truly no hope for a loss-making activity, get rid of it. But try everything else before taking this ultimate step. Internal reorganisation can amount to far less drastic action than divestment.

This introduction to the range of potential strategies has been brief and has concentrated on case studies illustrating how such strategies have been used in real-life situations in the recent past. Whichever is appropriate for your business, and whichever route you choose, you are about to enter the most complex part of the procedure – actually considering in detail the possible implications of specific action. Accordingly, the following four chapters analyse in depth the issues to which you should address yourself when determining specific action. Chapters 5 and 6 study closely the impact of generic growth on the business and the kind of internal reorganisation you may have to contemplate to cope with it. Chapter 7 examines the implications and questions inherent in a diversification-based strategy, while Chapter 8 examines the concept of growth by acquisition. The time for decisions is close at hand!

Chapter 5
Corporate Strategy and Generic Growth (1)

Whichever route to growth you select as your primary vehicle, it is likely that you will be looking for some increase in your existing activities. Only if you have decided to run down your present operation in favour of more profitable ways of spending your time, is this unlikely to be the case, and even here, you need to plan for a sensible, structured run-down of current activities which coincides with a gradual replacement by other ventures. In short, whichever way forward you select, you need to give strategic consideration to your plan's impact on your current activities and organisation. Further, if in full cognisance of the possibilities, you have selected generic growth as your optimal way forward, pretty well the whole of your planning will now be devoted to the implications of growth for the existing business. In most cases, the road ahead will consist of a fairly large slice of generic growth, a little flirting with diversification and possibly an acquisition tacked on if an appropriate one happens to catch the eye along the way. It's all to do with human nature, self-confidence, and a 'better the devil you know' attitude. Whatever the reason, the implication is that you as managing director have to think long and hard about the implications for your current business. Accordingly, this and the next chapter will concentrate on the means by which you can give life to your growth strategy and on the implications inherent in that strategy which you must take into account.

Growth and the achievement of strategic goals require:

- an information system capable of disclosing the state of the business and progress made at regular intervals;
- an organisational structure capable of coping with expansion;

- staff who are committed to the achievement of strategic goals.

Consequently, in addition to the mechanics of getting worthwhile growth, this chapter will examine the detailed requirements of the information system, organisational structure and personnel related considerations. Chapter 6 will look at the contribution approach to assessing your existing activities, your marketing strategy and the possibility of divestment of unprofitable segments of the business. Why these items in particular? Well, it was established in Chapter 3 that, in general, targets will tend to be set for financial and certain specific non-financial aspects of the business. The tools for achieving those targets will normally be the organisational structure, the marketing strategy and the monitoring (information) system. Get those in order and you've a much better chance of achieving your targets.

The management information systems

Whatever else may or may not be true with regard to the planning process in which you've engaged, it is certainly the case that you have very little hope of achieving strategic goals if you don't monitor progress towards them during the period of the plan by reference to interim targets. The three- or five-year targets should, ideally, first be broken down into annual budgets and to maximise the chances of achievement, those annual budgets need to be further subdivided into shorter periods again, preferably monthly. If you know where you're starting from, you then have detailed information relating to the improvements which have to be generated month by month to keep you on target for achieving the interim annual goal on the way to the strategic target. In addition, it will not be sufficient for a single company-wide target to be set at which 'we all have to aim', no matter how small you are. To stand a decent chance of success, periodic targets must be translated into personal targets.

A further bit of psychology becomes relevant here. If you simply share out your turnover targets among those responsible for gaining business, it only takes one of them to fail and the budget is blown. Everyone then faces the much more difficult task of gaining sufficient extra ground next month to make up for Mr Failure's shortfall this month. The answer? Individual sales targets should total more than 100 per cent of the month's budget. Then, if everyone pulls their weight and achieves targets, in aggregate you will do better than budget. If you're heavily commission-based, make sure that the really meaty commissions start being paid only when the budget is being well achieved.

All the emphasis so far has been on the subject of turnover. Of course, it is the natural inclination of most businessmen to home in on that turnover figure since it is work that keeps everyone occupied and the pennies rolling in. However, sales forecasts suffer from one major disadvantage. The best they can ever amount to is an intelligent guess. The good news though, is that virtually every other component of the profit budget should be far more accurately assessable in advance, which leads naturally to the key question in all this: just how sophisticated and detailed should the budget be? The only answer is that it should be as detailed as you have resources to make it. The more detailed your forecasts of what should happen, the more intelligent will be your analysis of actual results and explanations of any variance from the budget. It should be fairly obvious that the detail of budgeting applicable to a divisionalised conglomerate will be too sophisticated for the corner shop. But the time to worry is when you are the divisionalised conglomerate (or nearly so) and your budgeting procedures are not sophisticated or, indeed, when you are the corner shop and not doing any budgeting at all. It is difficult to be specific given the scale range of possibilities, but there seems no good reason why even the small business should not be able to budget to the level of detail indicated in Figures 3(a), (b) and (c). Of course, the detailed entries, layout and means of analysis are unique to each business and the best that can be offered here is a general indication of the sort of information which you should be looking for. However, a couple of general points will apply to virtually all situations:

1. Budgets to the gross profit level should be based on a planned product mix. It is not usually sufficient to estimate an overall turnover figure and apply a gross profit percentage that looks vaguely achievable in the context of historic performance. It is too easy to make excuses if things go wrong. More importantly, an aggregate approach makes it much harder to spot opportunities for easy improvement. Getting down to specific individual products gives you the opportunity of examining their performance in detail and getting the most mileage out of each one.

Figure 3(a). *Profit and loss account*

Smallco Bigideas Limited
Profit & Loss Account
Month _____

	Current Month			Year to Date		
	Actual	Budget	Variance	Actual	Budget	Variance
Total sales	192,750	175,000				
Total cost of sales	113,000	110,000				
Gross profit	79,750	65,000				
GP%	41.3%	37.1%				
Overheads						
Staff						
Salaries	10,000	10,000				
Vehicle costs	3,100	3,000				
Training	1,200	1,000				
Canteen	800	750				
	15,100	14,750				
Establishment						
Rent and rates	2,000	2,000				
Telephones and insurances	1,250	750				
Depreciation	1,500	1,500				
Light and heat	850	750				
	5,600	5,000				
Administration						
Advertising and promotion	900	1,000				
Printing, postage and stationery	300	350				
Periodicals	250	200				
Legal and professional	4,000	1,000				
Accountancy	500	500				
	5,950	3,050				
Finance						
Bank charges	125	100				
Loan interest	1,200	1,000				
	1,325	1,100				
Contingency	–	1,750				
Total overhead	27,975	25,650				
Net profit	51,775	37,600				
Net profit %	26.9%	21.4%				

Figure 3(b). *Turnover and gross profit budget*

Smallco Bigideas Limited
Turnover & Gross Profit Budget
Month _____

	Current Month			Year to Date		
	Actual	Budget	Variance	Actual	Budget	Variance
Product A						
Unit sales	10,500	10,000				
Unit price	9.5	10				
Turnover	99,750	100,000				
Direct labour	19,500	20,000				
Direct materials	31,000	30,000				
Direct other costs	5,250	5,000				
Cost of sales	55,750	55,000				
Gross profit Product A	44,000	45,000				
GP%	44.1%	45%				
Product B						
Unit sales	15,500	15,000				
Unit price	6	5				
Turnover	93,000	75,000				
Direct labour	18,500	18,000				
Direct materials	32,000	30,000				
Direct other costs	6,750	7,000				
Cost of sales	57,250	55,000				
Gross profit Product B	35,750	20,000				
GP%	38.4%	26.6%				
Gross profit all products	79,750	65,000				
GP%	41.3%	37.1%				

2. It was argued above that the hardest figure to assess accurately in advance is the one that matters most – turnover – and that virtually all the others ought to be much easier to forecast. Items such as those given as examples in Figure 3(a) ought to be relatively easy to guess at intelligently. Probably the most important one itemised is the last overhead figure, the contingency. It is there in recognition of human fallibility; you will not get every figure on that forecast right. Hopefully, most of the plusses and minuses will balance each other out but the contingency is there for the same reason that individual sales targets should total more than the company's target – to stop you blowing the budget. Both the contingency and the excess sales targets are items that should not assume great prominence in your thinking or they will become excuses for failure to hit targets, but they are necessary. Remember that the context of all this is a five-year corporate plan and you must do everything possible to ensure those targets are treated as minimum figures. In short, you should be looking for positive variances in both turnover and contingency. If you are not getting them, find out why.

The question inevitably arises as to why you have to go to all this trouble and expense (yes, it is actually going to cost you money) every month just to produce figures. The answer is that you are doing far more than simply seeing how well you did: you are providing yourself with the information you need to correct things that are going wrong before they go too far, and that is why it's important to monitor both monthly figures themselves and cumulative year to date achievements. For instance, if product A shows an adverse variance for one month, you may not worry too much. If it happens two months running the trend will show up in the cumulative figures and then you should start to be concerned – when you are dealing with five-year targets, trends are of enormous importance.

Better still, don't wait for an adverse trend to establish itself. If, in any given month, an actual figure is materially worse than the budgeted estimate, find out why and act to correct it. Assuming it is within the company control, the cause may be one of two possibilities: either there is an error on someone's part or the budget was unrealistic. If it is the former, find out who and why, get to the bottom of the problem and put it right. If the latter,

Figure 3(c). *Cash flow*

Smallco Bigideas Limited
Cash flow

	January		February	
	Actual	Budget	Actual	Budget
Receipts				
Cash from debtors	191,250	189,750		195,500
Other cash receipts	5,750	–		
Total cash receipts	197,000	189,750		195,500
Payments				
Cash to creditors	66,400	67,500		75,750
Wages, Salaries, NI	48,000	48,000		48,000
Vehicle costs	3,600	3,450		3,450
Training	850	1,150		1,150
Canteen costs	1,400	1,650		850
Rent & Rates				
Telephones & Insurances	7,250	6,500		
Light & Heat	4,250	3,600		
Advertising & Promotion	1,250	1,150		1,150
Printing, Postage &				
Stationery	350	400		400
Periodicals	230	230		230
Legal & Professional fees	1,150	1,150		1,150
Accountancy	–	–		6,900
VAT				
Operational cash payments	134,730	134,780		139,030
Net operational flow	62,270	54,970		56,470
Opening balance	(20,000)	(20,000)		34,970
Loan repayments				
Loan interest				
Interest & Charges				
Closing balance	42,270	34,970		91,440

March		April		May		June	
Actual	Budget	Actual	Budget	Actual	Budget	Actual	Budget
	190,750		207,000		212,750		218,500
	190,750		207,000		212,750		218,500
	82,500		87,500		92,000		96,000
	48,000		48,000		48,000		48,000
	3,450		3,450		3,450		3,450
	1,150		1,150		1,150		1,150
	850		850		850		850
	24,000		–		–		–
	1,150		1,150		1,150		1,150
	400		400		400		400
	230		230		230		230
	1,150		1,150		1,150		1,150
	–		3,400		–		–
			22,500				
	162,880		169,780		148,380		152,380
	27,870		37,220		64,370		66,120
	91,440		106,010		143,230		207,600
	(10,000)						(10,000)
	(3,000)						(3,000)
	(300)						(300)
	106,010		143,230		207,600		260,420

perhaps it is time to revise those budgets. Whatever you do, do not fail to act on information that you have gone to the trouble of providing – management control information is there to help you manage your business; if you don't use it you've no one else but yourself to blame.

There are good grounds for investigating material positive variances as well. Once again, they will arise for one of two reasons: either the budget has been set too conservatively or someone is doing better than expected. If it's a case of the former, once again flex that budget or it's of little use to you. However, if someone really is over-performing, that budget has served one of its most important purposes in helping you to identify who and reward that performance. And reward it you must. There is nothing that encourages people to perform well as much as appreciation, nor anything so demoralising as failure to appreciate.

So far, this analysis of management information systems has homed in only on profit and loss budgets and the uses they can be put to. However, there's more to corporate life than the profit and loss account, in particular, balance sheets and cash. In Chapter 2, a number of questions were posed which may have caused you to take a long, hard look at your balance sheet (true value of assets and liabilities, days' sales in debtors and days' purchases in creditors etc).

Assuming that you have a system sufficiently sophisticated to produce all this information, the danger is in concentrating on the profit and loss account and ignoring the rest. If you have never calculated days' sales in debtors, do so now (it is easily done – divide sales for the period by days in the period, then divide debtors at the end of the period by the result). The result can be eyebrow-raising; do your customers really take an average of 90 days to pay you? The preservation of customer relations is one thing, but that excessive payment period is costing you hard cash in terms of overdraft interest actually paid or deposit interest forgone, depending on the cash position you are in.

So, where does this leave you? First, needing to calculate all those ratios (see Appendix 3 for the formulae) and second, monitoring them on a regular basis. Not surprisingly, the easiest way to do that is to extend your budget profit and loss account into budget cash flow and balance sheet, record actual figures and explore the reasons for variances. This is getting pretty much into the accountant's province, and certainly, if you have one, get him to do the calculations for you. If there is no accountant in the house and you are not confident of your ability to do the budgeting, grit your teeth and spend some money on a professional. It will be well-spent, since it is utterly pointless trying to measure performance by a budget in which no one has any faith.

It is not the function of this text to provide a detailed treatise on management information systems (or, for that matter, any other technical tool you may use for the achievement of strategic goals), but rather to convince of the need for a competent system to keep track of progress. However, one or two logical conclusions (which may be fairly obvious) need to be pointed out. First, if you intend to have a sophisticated (or nearly so) budgeting system, it must sit on top of a total information-gathering system that is capable of producing reliable information from basic invoices and stock takes upwards. Don't forget that you should be monitoring monthly or recording stock continuously if you want to produce meaningful results. Hence, the systems that feed into budget and actual results need to be as good as the monthly accounts themselves or they will drag the latter down with them. No doubt the pound signs are starting to appear in the eyes of the more astute reader and, yes, unfortunately, quality costs money. But if you are going to do it at all, you might as well do it right. If you do not get the recording system right you are unlikely to make corporate planning work (doesn't this give you a feeling of *déjà vu*?). Of course, one factor that tends to make it much easier these days is the advent of the trusty micro-computer and the faithful old spread sheet programme. Profit and loss, cash flow and balance sheet models can all be set up relatively easily on a spread sheet, leaving you only to plug in the figures while the machine does the donkey work of making the calculations.

The second fairly obvious conclusion is that all this information is rather too much for one poor MD, sitting in his office, to absorb. The answer to the problem is clearly, therefore, to be very selective with regard to who is responsible for acting on what information. Ideally, the board should receive monthly accounts ten working days after the month end (if US subsidiaries can achieve this, why can't you?), together with a full report on the figures. Those responsible for variances should be ready with explanations and proposals for immediate remedial action if appropriate. It's what management by exception and objective is all about.

If all this sounds a little like pie in the sky and a bit too much for your poor team to stomach, just remember that technology has provided us with that most wondrous of inventions, the computer. While there may be a grain of truth in the old adage that 'it takes a computer to really foul things up', if used properly, they can save a remarkable amount of time. And while this text is not intended to be a businessman's guide to computers, it suffices to say that you should be able to get a very serviceable system for rather less than you spend on the Jag (OK, so you can't drive a computer, but you can fly one; try the flight simulators – they're enormous fun).

Where does all this leave you? Certainly with the conclusion that if you are going for generic growth, you must have an information system capable of disclosing your progress frequently, accurately, and speedily to give you the information you need to keep you on course. If you have no system, now is the time to think about installing one.

It has been concluded so far that the purpose of the management information system is to give you regular, timely information to enable you to assess the progress of the business towards your stated targets. It has also been established that the purpose of the budget with which you compare your actual results is to ensure that you make regular, measured progress towards the medium-term objective that you have set. But that budget does have one other very important task, and that is to ensure that each part of the plan is both feasible and consistent with every other part of the plan.

When you first attempt to establish five-year goals, you will, naturally, do so largely by rule of thumb. Examine them in a little more depth and, in particular, in the context of departmental budgets and you may find a whole host of problems that you never anticipated. Global turnover targets have to translate eventually into sales budgets for individual products. Question: are those budgets feasible in the context of sales of those products that have previously been achieved? Sales targets will also have a direct implication for production budgets and proposed stock levels. Question: does the production department have the physical capacity to achieve the proposed production levels? If not, are we talking about expanding production capacity, additional shifts, overtime working or what? Whichever route you choose, it will cost you, so make sure those costs are reflected adequately in the budget. Also, make sure that the people who will have to carry out the policy are party to the decision taking and the establishment of the targets. Failure to do so spells trouble. In addition, don't forget that additional sales and production imply additional procurement and stocking costs. It should be someone's responsibility to ensure that suppliers do not create bottlenecks that will blow your budgets. And, to make the point for the umpteenth time, it's at times like these that you'll be glad you went for second sourcing. As far as stocks are concerned, you'll be carrying more in all probability; don't forget the working capital and cash implications, or overtrading will get you in the end.

Getting the growth

If there's one central point fundamental to the argument of this book it's that there's little point in going for growth unless you plan it. Hitting all the sales targets in the world will do you no good at all unless:

- the price gives you the margin you need to hit profit targets;
- you have the physical capacity, materials, labour and organisation you need to deliver the goods on time;
- your working capital is adequate to finance the period between the payments you make and the payments you get.

Although this book is about planning and emphatically not about sales, so far one very important question has been largely begged: how do you get the sales that amount to growth? When the organisation is there, the budgeting has been done, the capacity and working capital are organised and the marketing is under way, to get the growth you have to get out there and sell. Marketing, production planning and, ultimately, corporate strategy itself have essentially one purpose only: to create in your company an environment that is conducive to growth. But if you do not put the effort into selling, that growth will not be forthcoming.

What you have to do to achieve sales will depend enormously on the type of business you're in. The sales strategy for a manufacturing company with a large sales force will, for obvious reasons, differ markedly from that of a proprietor-run fast food retailer. However, a number of features will be common to inducing sales regardless of the environment. While it again needs to be emphasised that this is not a sales manual, no text on corporate planning can really be complete without examining at

81

least some of the more fundamental aspects of sales upon which corporate growth will depend.

- Remember that you are not selling a customer a product or service. You are selling him the satisfaction of a want or a need that he perceives himself to have. Identify specifically what that need is, match the attributes of your product to it and you have a customer. In particular, identify the ways in which his current supplier is failing to meet his needs and make sure that he knows you can do better.

- The satisfaction of a need does not lie wholly in the product itself. Whether it's a photocopier or a hamburger, it must be delivered within a reasonable time-scale, courteously and in a state capable of fulfilling the need that it was purchased to satisfy. Consequently, you must be aware that you are selling not just a particular product but a whole range of peripheral services that contribute towards the satisfaction of the need.

- There are very few products that people buy only once, so get it right and you should have a customer who returns to you when the need arises again. Of course, there are a very large number of businesses which rely greatly on repeat trade. It all adds up to giving the customer what he expects and, if appropriate, more than he expects to ensure that his need is satisfied. In addition, you always have the possibility of selling the satisfied customer other products in your range. The dissatisfied customer is not likely to go on buying from you for very long.

The question of doing more than is expected is also worthy of clarification – going the second mile can win you a friend for life. Let a personal story illustrate. I once needed some minor crash damage repaired on my car. As normal, I obtained a number of quotes and told the insurance company which I would prefer to accept and why. They agreed and the car was duly delivered for the work to be carried out. When I returned a few days later, not only had a good repair job been done but the car had been cleaned inside and out and polished as well. Needless to say, when I next needed some damage repaired, there was only one place I wanted to take the car. By contrast, I arranged with another firm for a hire car to be available while my own car was off the road. Not only was it half an hour late in being delivered, it was also not the model I had requested. Reasonable explanations were forthcoming for both points, but I have never felt inclined to hire another car from that organisation.

You may have all the good reasons that there are for failure to perform, and for a while you may be able to rely on most people being reasonably tolerant, but eventually, if you can't do the job and someone else can, you cannot expect to retain the customer. Quite reasonably, people want results, not excuses.

All the above point to the way in which you do a job or provide a product once you have a customer, but the hardest part of the exercise is getting the customer in the first place. In addition, growth must amount to two things: continuing to supply existing customers once you have them and obtaining new ones. An element of growth may be attributable to supplying more of the same to current customers but unless their need is expanding rapidly, you are unlikely to achieve your own growth targets without obtaining new business. By now, it should come as no surprise that the process of obtaining new customers can be as much the subject of a strategic approach as any other part of the business. Indeed, failure to treat it as such exposes it to exactly the same dangers as any other aspect of the operation for which you do not plan.

Getting new customers starts with a co-ordinated marketing policy, designed to get your name and image established in the market-place. (For details of a strategic approach to marketing see Chapter 6.) If properly constructed, the marketing process should result in direct enquiries. Those direct enquiries should be followed up by the sales force, trained for the purpose and bearing in mind the points of principle enumerated above. Sales enquiries lead to sales, sales to production, production to delivery and delivery to cash. Assuming that you have an averagely good sales force, performing at an average level, use of the motivational techniques set out earlier should alone lead to better sales performance.

Once the slack has been taken up, the only way to expand sales will be by additional effort to convert leads into sales, additional effort to generate more sales and, in due course, the employment of more salesmen. Once again, emphasising the potential impact on strategy, most sales people can be helped to perform better by a change in perception of exactly what their function comprises. Most see their job as converting leads given to them by someone else into sales. Now, consider the potential impact on sales if every salesman personally generated an additional lead for every sale he made. The matter can be as simple as asking the customer whether there's anyone else in the organisation that the salesman should see, or even anyone else outside the organisation known to the customer who might be interested in buying. And this is really where the fundamental conceptual points made earlier have greatest impact. If you've satisfied a customer he will be much keener to introduce you to other potential customers than if he's not happy with you. There aren't many firms in any given industry that go to the trouble of delivering more satisfaction than required. Be one of them and your future will be rosier.

But what if the marketing strategy has failed to produce the leads that you're looking for? First, question whether you've got it right, but after that consider whether you should be taking the mountain to Mohammed. There are some industries where cold calling is simply impractical (retailing for example) but others where a telephone enquiry can work wonders. However, a couple of warnings are appropriate. First, cold telephone canvassing doesn't tend to go down too well with Joe Public – a telephone call in the middle of the evening meal is not the best way to start a sale. There ought to be more imaginative ways of reaching the consumer than by telephone or leaflets which don't get read. Just because the flock do it that way doesn't mean you should follow blindly, and if you do, you may deserve the same fate as the other sheep. Getting fleeced! Second, if you are going to use telephone canvassing, make sure you use experienced people who don't sound as though they're reading a prepared script (even if they are!) and choose the telephone numbers intelligently – don't just work down the page.

Finally, to summarise, no corporate strategy is complete without a sales strategy. Indeed, some business watchers are of the opinion that corporate strategy amounts to marketing strategy. By now you should be convinced that there is, in fact, more to it than that but lest you run the risk of overemphasising sales, consider the following example.

In 1980, some salesmen of a computer company in west London decided they wanted to work for themselves. They were all of the opinion that it was sales and only sales that made business tick and because they understood sales their business was guaranteed to succeed. Well, in terms of sales they were successful. Turnover hit break-even levels from the first month and was destined to rise steeply for each of the next four years.

But somehow the company never seemed to sort out its

administrative problems. It never invoiced as promptly as it could have done and the chasing of debtors wasn't as quick as it should have been. The business hit cash flow problems from its earliest days, not because its original capital base was too low nor even because it was overtrading. It was simply that the primary response to every problem was to sell more product. The fundamental assumption was that if there were difficulties, it was because turnover was too low. It was some time before the directors called on outside expertise to help solve the problem. The real solution lay in improving cash flow, organising administration along more efficient lines and installing a computer to do the invoicing rather more promptly than the manual systems had permitted. The moral of the story? Of course, without sales you do not have a company – but sales on their own are never enough.

Organisational structure

It's now time to make the conceptual jump from merely defining the structure that you currently have, to developing one that is best for the business and most conducive to the achievement of the growth targets that you've now adopted. However, it's also necessary to reiterate the warning raised in Chapter 2 – when you decide to change the organisational structure of the business, take careful account of the vested interests that have developed over the years. Take one very small example by way of illustration. A small high technology company in Yorkshire had grown gradually over a number of years from little more than a one-man band to a reasonably substantial organisation. The marketing director had an assistant who had coped reasonably well for most of the period but was showing obvious signs of strain as the workload built up. Nevertheless, he was the director's assistant and drew all his status from the fact. Eventually, the director himself decided he needed more help than his assistant was able to give and recruited a new PA. The resentment caused was instant and dramatic. The assistant felt he had been demoted after years of loyal service and the tension between him and the PA was obvious for all to see. Eventually, a solution was cobbled together whereby he worked for someone else within the business.

The moral of the story is this: if such a small and innocuous matter as the appointment of a new PA can cause this degree of resentment, consider the possible impact of organisational changes on established relationships and patterns of work within your business. You might be forgiven for concluding that it isn't worth making changes in view of the aggro you will generate by doing so and, indeed, it's certainly better to grow along predetermined structured lines from the start if this is possible. However, if you honestly conclude that the good of the business requires structural and responsibility changes, you serve no one's interests and least of all your own, by failing to make them. The question then largely becomes one of how to make the changes with the minimum denting of self-esteem. Don't forget that everyone within the organisation needs to maintain self-respect.

So how do you determine whether the organisational structure is all that it should be? First, in some cases, it will be blatantly obvious that it is not and if you fall into this category you will be aware of it! Beyond that though, the primary question to ask is, 'Does the organisational structure you currently have optimise contribution to the strategic targets you have set?' Organisational structure is essentially a matter of responsibility – who in the business is responsible for what. You have to answer the question of optimal contribution to strategic goals by looking at the key individuals within the business and determining whether each is in the best position to make that optimal contribution. For instance, do the areas of activity allocated to any one individual place him in the position of having conflicting responsibilities? Have you fallen foul of the temptation to place too many responsibilities on the most capable people in the business? While individuals who show ability and promise will normally thrive on additional responsibility, they must be able to delegate their less responsible tasks to others or you're in danger of having nothing done properly.

For each individual within the organisation, for each set of responsibilities allocated to a job title, examine them within the context of strategic goals and determine whether what you have established will permit those goals to be achieved. If a given sales manager is responsible for two products and sales of each are anticipated to expand rapidly, will he cope? If you're considering giving one individual (yourself included) primary responsibility for an acquisition, how will he cope with his existing workload? There is obviously a reluctance to rush out and employ more people until you're confident that expansion is coming as anticipated but somewhere there lies a balance point between overloading people until the last possible moment and having new people underemployed while you wait for the expansion to come. That balance point you will have to establish in the light of your development towards your strategic goals. In essence, the key point is this: ensure that the organisational structure you evolve is in keeping with and contributes to the strategic targets that you have set. If not, rectification at a later stage will come expensive – and may come too late.

Of course, if you're in the early stages of corporate life, it is entirely possible that little organisational structure will yet have emerged within your business and certainly, some people will be wearing several hats. You may therefore be in a position of enormous potential advantage in that you are now giving consideration to how you can best direct the development of your structure to avoid the difficulties which beset the business that has grown along unstructured lines. The essence of getting it right lies in determining the structure which will best support the growth targets you have set and ensuring that each area of responsibility that you subsequently allocate takes you towards your planned structure. You must simply not permit custom and practice to grow up in conflict with the structure you need to serve your strategic targets.

Personnel

This chapter has so far examined some of the key aspects of the business that need to work smoothly if you are to achieve strategic targets through generic growth, ie doing more of what you do now. No examination can be considered complete without some attention being paid to the people who make it possible for you to do business – your staff. There is a very real sense in which the whole of this book is about people, and the heavy emphasis it lays on personnel is no accident. You cannot determine where the business is currently nor plan strategic targets nor set routes for their achievement without realistic consideration of the impact of those decisions on the people who have to actuate them. That is why the point has repeatedly been made that individuals should be involved in the decisions that affect their working lives as fundamentally as strategic decisions are bound to do.

The simple involvement of individuals in the planning process is not adequate consideration as far as personnel are concerned. How did you answer the questions in Chapter 2 which related to personnel? Whether directed at key individuals within the workforce or at the workforce as a whole, the questions were all aimed in essentially the same direction. How do you get the best out of the people who work for you? A considerable amount has already been said on the subject of goal congruence, ie making sure that employees are working towards the same objectives as have been set for the company. But assuming that you have arrived at that blissful state of harmony and all is well with the world, what next? The key objective, the key contribution that personnel can make to the achievement of strategic targets, is to ensure that everyone is doing their utmost to serve the interests of the company. To get to those strategic goals, you need the best people, committed to the company's targets and giving their best for the achievement of those targets.

Attention has already been devoted to the psychology of target setting – how ambitious to be and how much to involve people. But suppose that you've taken on board all the advice expounded within these covers; suppose you've got goal congruence; suppose you've set the targets psychologically correctly: what happens if you've got it all right and either individuals, groups or the company as a whole still aren't hitting the targets? Voicing generalities as to the cause is dangerous but at least start by considering the following:

- if the whole company's off target, it's probably the target which is wrong;
- if a particular segment of the company's off target, it may well be that the management of that segment is at fault;
- if individuals are off target, the chances are that the individuals are at fault.

Considerable attention has already been focused on the first two of these areas; getting the target right and managing for its achievement. But what do you do when you have a genuine case of an individual apparently personally at fault? People's natural reactions vary from the 'off with his head' approach of instant dismissal to the manager who will bend over backwards not to lose an employee. The best advice that can be offered here is to move cautiously – things are rarely all that they seem on the surface. Before taking irrevocable action, make sure you've got to the root of the problem. If there are extenuating circumstances which will change, think seriously whether it's worth going to all the trouble of dismissal and reappointment, particularly if the individual potentially has a serious contribution to make to the organisation. And just bear one thing in mind: every individual is unique and consequently has a unique contribution to make to your business. Give him his cards and you've lost forever that contribution which he could have made. You must think long and hard before throwing away something unique – by definition, you'll never get an exact replacement.

Getting the best out of people amounts to motivation and motivation comes from understanding how people think. Beyond the pay packet lies a vast, often untapped reservoir of personal commitment that you can engender for your business. If all this sounds like yet more repetition on the theme of getting the best out of people, it's because it's the most important theme of this book. Perhaps it's something to do with national character. Try the following case study.

In the mid-1970s a Swiss businessman decided to set up in the UK. He disposed of his interests abroad, moved his family here and set up in specialist plastic coatings in Scotland. He took a Scottish Development Agency factory and employed local labour. Over the next ten years, the business faced the normal range of ups and downs until in 1983 some legislative changes raised demand for the product dramatically and the company's future was assured. But the most interesting feature of the business was this: in the whole of its history not only did the company face no industrial dispute of any kind whatsoever, but also the whole of the workforce was totally committed to its success. Why? Possibly because the wage packets tended to be a little larger than average and perhaps because the working conditions were good, but what it really had to do with was the personal involvement that the MD took in the practical side of the business, even down to working on the production line and packing the product when the pressure was on – and there aren't too many British MDs you'll ever see doing that.

Summary

The purpose of this chapter and the one that follows is to highlight some of the key components of the business to which you must give consideration in order to ensure that generic growth has the maximum chance of taking you to your strategic targets as set. But it should be emphasised again that this text does not purport to be a detailed treatise on any of the matters raised here or in Chapter 6. If you have a particular problem with any area examined, first try reading a specialist text on the subject and then, if necessary, consult an expert. The principal points made in this chapter have been:

1. The achievement of strategic goals through generic growth will require a competent information system, a structured organisation and staff committed to the targets.
2. The information system should be capable of producing reasonably accurate management accounts on a monthly basis within ten working days of the month end (and it may well be worth sacrificing a degree of accuracy for speed in this case).
3. Individual targets should total more than 100 per cent of budget and the budget should include a contingency.
4. When all the planning is finished and the machine is fully primed and ready to go, actually getting that growth will depend on making sales. Don't forget that you are selling the satisfaction of a need and that some of your business will be repeat business, so create customer loyalty.
5. Make sure that your organisation structure is conducive to the achievement of your strategic goals – but if you plan to change an existing structure, bear in mind that you're dealing with people's self-esteem and tread as on eggs.
6. Without wishing to repeat this *ad infinitum*, just bear in mind that people are unique individuals.

Thus, the information system, sales, organisational structure and people are all necessary working components of your growth strategy, but on their own they are not sufficient. For further components, turn to Chapter 6.

Chapter 6
Corporate Strategy and Generic Growth (2)

Lest you run the risk of losing sight of the woods while studying the pine needles, take some time now to examine the road that you have travelled so far. The pursuit of the gold at the end of the corporate rainbow started from the argument that it was important that you plan the future of your business for a number of reasons: to stand the best possible chance of getting to a stated destination and to avoid business failure, to ensure all in the organisation are pulling in the same direction and to measure the progress you're making. The second step in the argument went something along the lines that there isn't much point in planning unless you know where you're starting from, hence you should set out a reasoned analysis of where the business is now with regard to all its constituent parts and policies. Third, having ensured an adequate working knowledge of where you are now (and it's surprising how many businessmen do not fully appreciate the current circumstances within their businesses), it is feasible to consider setting the targets that you can expect to achieve over an extended time horizon of three or five years.

You are likely to want to establish both overall financial targets for the organisation as a whole and other, probably non-financial targets for constituent parts of the business, particularly to avoid perceived problems, correct sub-optimal conditions and create a machine capable of achieving your global goals. But other than rectifying specific conditions you have perceived to be weak and acting to pre-empt difficulties, you still have to decide as a matter of general policy how you mean to arrive at your intended destination. There are three main ways to achieve growth, with a fourth subsidiary route applicable in a limited number of situations: you can raise the level of your existing activities, but take care not to overtrade and beware the theory that says 'more

91

of the same is the safest way'; you can diversify; you can acquire other businesses; or you can reorganise existing activities to lower overheads and ultimately divest yourself of unwanted or unprofitable activities.

In the next few chapters, each of these possibilities will be examined in turn, though not exhaustively, since it would be easy to devote a volume to each. Chapter 5 turned the spotlight on a number of key factors that need to be considered when following generic growth in pursuit of strategic targets. Since it is likely that any corporate strategy will depend on growth of existing activities and internal reorganisation, whatever other options are available, this chapter will highlight some further specific areas within the organisation that may need attention, in particular:

- using a contribution approach to management accounting;
- marketing;
- divestment of unprofitable operations.

Contribution

Apart from the obvious question, 'What is it?', a number of very reasonable questions naturally arise concerning the use of a contribution approach to accounting, such as, 'This is no textbook on accounting, so why consider it at all?' and 'If you have to bore us with this, why didn't you raise it back in Chapter 5 when you dealt with management information systems?' To answer the questions in reverse order, the concept of contribution, although related to the way in which you present your monthly management accounts, is conceptually distinct from the management information system. It's dealt with here because it's probably the most significant contribution that accountancy can make to both profit generation (as opposed to measurement) and corporate strategy itself. As for what it is, read on.

First, it is (once again) not possible to do the subject justice in a few hundred words, so go to the trouble and enormous expense of buying a recognised accountancy text that deals with it properly. But get to grips with it you should, because it's a fundamentally important tool for establishing the individual profitability of the products you produce in relation to those expensive resources used in their production. The theory goes something along these lines. You can divide all the costs incurred in your organisation between those that are fixed over a period of time (like rates, say) and those that vary depending on your volume of production (like raw materials). The ones that vary (variable costs) can be allocated to the products that you actually produce. The difference between the price at which you sell the product and the variable cost you incurred in its production is the contribution of the product towards fixed costs and profits. Knowing what that contribution is gives you a powerful tool in the control of your business. It tells you how much product you have to sell at a given price to cover your costs, how much profit you will make on a given level of production and what the impact will be on profit of a change in any of the variables you face – selling price variable costs or overhead. Take a simple example:

The Widget Manufacturing Company Ltd produces only one product, the red, semi-detached, three-legged widget (RSTW), which is in great demand. The company operates a contribution approach to accounting and knows the following data apply:

	£	£
Selling price per unit		200
Variable costs per unit		
Materials	20	
Labour	50	
Overhead	30	100
Contribution		100
Annual fixed overhead	£1,000,000	

Thus, for each RSTW sold for £200, variable costs of £100 are incurred, leaving a contribution to fixed overheads of £100. If the company correctly understands itself to face £1,000,000 of fixed overheads this year, it must obviously sell 10,000 RSTWs to cover its costs and break even. Further, for each unit over 10,000 that it sells, it makes £100 profit, because the overheads have been covered by the contribution of the first 10,000 units. So long as the relationships hold true, the company can budget profitability for any level of output and sales that it can achieve. But even in the one-product company, it's possible to go further than this. For any change in any element in the equation, you can predict both quickly and accurately the impact on profit and determine the action that will most effectively counter the difficulty. For instance, if there's a wage rise and labour per unit now costs 10 per cent more, contribution per unit falls to £95. Now let's suppose that the budget was for sales of 1,000 RSTWs per month, 12,000 per year with a budget profit of £200,000 (12,000 × £100 contribution less £1,000,000 overheads). If the company takes no action at all, profit will fall to £140,000 (ie 12,000 × £95 − £1,000,000). There are four lines of defence if budget profit is to be maintained:

- cut overheads;
- increase price and maintain unit sales;
- maintain price and increase unit sales;
- reduce other variable costs.

Which of those routes the company takes will depend on the unique situation in which it finds itself. Cutting overheads is probably the least likely course of action, since in the efficiently managed company these should be running at a minimum in any case. Further cuts may mean changing the Jag for a Metro, and that's going to be painful. The condition of the market will determine whether it's possible to raise price or output and if the product is in strong demand, either of these might be feasible. Increased output means expanding your share of the market, which may mean hard work, but raising prices will incur customer resistance.

While we're on the subject of price, it's interesting to note that to some degree, almost all companies treat it as a variable to be manipulated to maximise sales without appreciating the true impact of price cuts on profitability. It's very widely used as a defensive measure in the face of a contracting market. Yet what the price cutters fail to realise is that if you do reduce price you have to work harder to sell increased volume into a contracting market to maintain profit − you're running ever harder just to stay in the same place. The crucial figures are contribution, unit sales and overhead. Unless you marry the three together, you will not be profitable no matter how much you manipulate price.

The corollary of all this is the impact that a price increase can have on contribution and consequently profit. The price effect is actually magnified into the contribution figure. In the above example, a 5 per cent increase with no change in sales level or variable cost would result in a 10 per cent increase in contribution and, on sales of 12,000 units, a 60 per cent increase in net profit!

Now just think. How much increased effort would you have to put in to make that 5 per cent price increase stick? Far less in all probability than the effort you would have to put in to find new markets to sell the 160 extra units (13 per cent) into.

It should be obvious by now that when you adopt a contribution approach to management accounts, you are able to home in much more clearly on the figures that matter. Let it be clearly stated that contribution or variable cost accounting can be a complex science and a field in which a little knowledge is undoubtedly a dangerous thing. Bear in mind, in particular, the complexities that will arise if you apply it to the multi-product company, especially if one or more resources (labour, materials etc) is in limited supply. If you're in any doubt at all as to your ability to modify the management information system to produce accounts in this format, call in an accountant – it will be well worth your while.

Marketing

Marketing, in essence, amounts to a process whereby you create the right environment in the market-place for the profitable sale of your products. While sales promotion is an important element in the marketing process, marketing is not sales nor can marketing effort replace sales effort in the final event. You still have to get out there in the market-place and persuade the buyer to do the buying, but the point of the marketing process is to create in the mind of the buyer an awareness of several points:

1. He needs widgets.
2. You are the best widget manufacturer to buy from.
3. Your widgets are the best on the market for his particular needs.

It is with particular reference to the last of these that you need to establish clearly which sector of the market each of your products addresses, so that the marketing and promotional effort can be directed at establishing your widgets as clearly the best in that sector.

The extent to which each of these three points is applicable will depend very largely on the kind of market in which you function, as will the specific marketing effort you undertake. In a new market you will have to work harder at 1 because the market-place may be unaware of the existence of the product and the benefits that it can offer. In the case of a highly competitive market 2 and 3 will need additional emphasis, since you'll be out there shouting alongside everyone else to be heard. In a market with very little competition 1 and 2 tend to run at a low level in the background while the emphasis is on 3 to keep reminding the market of what you can do for it.

But what should your marketing effort consist of, and how does it fit into what we're really here to talk about, the corporate plan?

First, as emphasised in Chapter 2, you can't have a corporate plan without a marketing plan. Some would go as far as to say that if you have a good marketing strategy you can forget the rest. Hopefully the arguments in the preceding pages will have convinced you that this is not quite true and that corporate planning means planning for the whole of the business. Nevertheless, it remains true that marketing planning is fundamental to the successful implementation of the corporate plan and, as with the rest of the plan, it's not enough to write it, implement it and forget it.

Marketing, like planning in general, is a living, developing process that needs constant monitoring, constant refining, constant attention. What actually comprises that plan and the action that subsequently arises from it will depend (yet again) on the market environment in which you function.

The promotional techniques of many producers are well known, ranging from newspaper advertising and mail shots to telephone canvassing and free competitions. For the MD convinced of the value of corporate and market planning it is essential to avoid at all costs simply doing what the others do just exactly because they *are* doing it. One look at the success rate would be enough to convince you that there should be a better way! Unfortunately, the only means of revealing it is to sit down and think the whole sales and marketing process through, to look at past successes and failures, to think creatively about possible future action and where necessary to take expert professional advice.

There is, in fact, no substitute for going through the full marketing planning process. You have to look at your product, its pricing, the market-place it addresses and the means by which you promote it. In most cases, that means starting with a proper market audit to establish clearly what the market really wants and then planning for the provision of that product.

Unfortunately, the facts of life are that all this requires time, effort and expense (now where have you heard that before?).

When you're trying to come up with something unique to yourself and possibly conceptually new there's no substitute for starting from first principles. The whole marketing and sales process takes place along the following lines:

- through marketing investigation and planning you become aware of a market need which your distinctive abilities are capable of supplying;
- a market ignorant of the existence of you and your product is sensitised to your presence;
- it's made specifically aware of your products and their characteristics;
- direct contact is made with individual potential purchasers at a non-specific level;
- this non-specific contact is used to generate a specific interface between seller and buyer;
- a sale results;
- the product performs;
- a reputation is established which reinforces awareness of your presence.

There are stages in this process that will undoubtedly not apply to some market-places and perhaps others relating to other markets that have been omitted, but in essence the process is reasonably defined for most markets. The task for the MD and corporate planning team is to put some specific flesh on the bones of each stage and determine what exactly ought to be done by whom and when.

For instance, general market awareness might be generated by advertising in trade magazines. But how much better if it were done by editorial rather than advertising? (There is a somewhat strange but clearly observable phenomenon whereby intelligent people who don't necessarily believe all they are told in an advertisement will swallow editorial hook, line and space filler – because in many journals that's what editorial amounts to.) Most editors are only too glad to carry space filling text, and if they won't, how about an advertising feature? If you pay for the space you can write what you like within reason, although it may be the case that advertising isn't the best medium for getting known at all. Many companies undertake it defensively – everyone else is doing it so we must – without ever assessing the benefits of the expenditure or evaluating the cost of refraining from it.

Undoubtedly, the best means to inform a market is by word of mouth and if you can do your sales promotion this way it's free as well. Admittedly for a large organisation in a diversified market it's unlikely to be adequate, but for a new business in a single location it's very well worth considering. How do you achieve it? Again, it depends largely on the business you're in, but for, say, a new firm of accountants in a county town, you could do worse than lunch all the local bank managers. Anyone who's lived a while in a given locality will have built up contacts. List them and spend some time with each establishing their contacts. Contact their contacts and make them aware of who you are and what you do. Bear in mind the corporate image that you're trying to create for the business and make sure that the points you emphasise are consistent with that image.

Finally, the point that's missed virtually every time – for every sale made or contract signed or whatever, ask the customer if he knows of anyone else who would be interested in you and your products. Let it be emphasised that this is only one very specific example of promotional effort that may be a little outside the normal approach of the rest of the herd.

When it comes to sales promotion planning for your company, the most valuable tool you have is that team you put together to write the corporate strategy with you. Use it as a think tank to come up with ideas unique to your situation. You may eventually conclude that your strategy should include some of the activities traditionally undertaken in your market-place – and don't go to the other extreme of rejecting media simply because they are in common use. The aim is to arrive at a systematic plan to get you and the right products known in the market-place and any process that cost-effectively achieves that end is worth considering seriously.

If generating turnover is a problem to you there are two or possibly three other points in the process where you may be deficient: moving from general awareness to specific contact, converting contacts into sales and, possibly, ensuring that sales establish reputation, market awareness and repeat purchases. If the problem lies in generating the specific contact, then there are two possible points of deficiency: either the promotional effort is not effective and the market is insufficiently aware of you, or you are failing to follow up the effort adequately and so generate the contact. If it's a case of the former, it's time to rethink your promotional activity. However, if it's the latter, it's time someone made the effort to contact more of those potential customers you've gone to such trouble to sensitise to your existence.

Converting contacts into sales is a much more definable problem. Determine what your contact/conversion ratio actually is. In many cases this will be quite low, say one in five or ten. Improving that conversion ratio can have a dramatic effect on your business. Suppose you currently find that for every 100 contacts you make 20 sales. If you could improve your conversion ratio by only five percentage points you face a potential increase in turnover of 25 per cent – and that could have a very large impact on the achievement of your corporate plan. Most people tend to concentrate simply on alternative ways to contact more potential customers in order to increase sales. Possibly, just possibly, you don't need any more contacts, merely an improvement in the converson ratio. Yet again, the solution will vary from one situation to another. Take the small South London building company previously referred to. Their conversion ratio was 20 per cent. Simply by following up tenders more promptly and regularly it was raised to 23 per cent implying an obvious improvement in turnover and less tendering time wasted as well. Enough said.

Suppose the problem lies in establishing reputation and repeat purchases once the sale is made. If you've got problems here there's something fundamentally wrong. Customers who place repeat orders make life so much easier. In most cases the most difficult element in the whole business process is establishing a regular customer. Give him what he wants and he'll tend to come back on his own, time after time; in fact, you will have to work quite hard to drive him away. We're all creatures of habit and view change as more risky than consistency. So if you're losing regular established customers there's something radically wrong and you should act quickly to find out why. Interestingly, most businessmen will go to great lengths to court new customers, with meals, conferences, days at the races etc, but how far do they go to court existing customers? Maybe you simply assume that if they've always bought from you they always will, but that's a dangerous and short-sighted assumption. Yes, you rightly put considerable effort into generating new business, but don't let it be at the cost of neglecting existing customers. If you've got valued regular customers then go to some trouble to show them they're important to you. And most important of all make sure that the product or service you provide is seen to be satisfying the customers' need. Let your customers know they're valued and maximise the quality of the product. Keep both constantly under review and reputation and repeat business will be assured.

If it's possible to single out one part of the business process as being most important, it's got to be marketing. Get everything else right and marketing wrong and you're wasting your time; but even if all other parts of the process leave something to be desired and you've got the marketing strategy right you'll generate profitable sales. To illustrate the significance of marketing, take a couple of examples from opposite ends of the spectrum.

Someone who had for many years been a civil servant decided that he wanted to go into business on his own. Because of his lack of commercial experience he decided that the safest way forward was to take on a franchise in photographic development. This he duly did and opened his doors to trade . . . and waited. Being a reserved sort of person he wasn't keen on the idea of actually going out and selling himself and his business to potential customers, so he just went on waiting. Eighteen months later he was still waiting. Apart from a small amount of business that had drifted in simply because he was there, he'd done virtually no trading. It hadn't helped that he'd had problems with his equipment and didn't feel confident that he'd be able to deliver the goods if he got the orders. It didn't help that he never really got the support from the franchise company that he was led to expect was available. Fundamentally the problem was that the customers never really came through the door – and that was because no one had ever gone out of his way to tell them that the doors were open and the service was there to be bought.

By contrast, and right at the other end of the scale, take the approach of the mighty IBM. IBM is well known as the epitome of the marketing-led corporation and there are many, many examples that could be drawn to confirm the point. By way of illustration, go back a decade or two to see the long-term consistency of the company's dedication to marketing strategy and the way it's repeatedly proved willing to move corporate mountains to keep up with the market. Interestingly, IBM was a relatively late entrant into the world of business computers, preferring not to be first or innovative but rather to see what the market demanded and then do it better than anyone else.

It was this strategy that by 1976 had gained it an overwhelmingly dominant position in the business mainframe market. In an uneducated market where most buyers were computer-illiterate

IBM offered the total service – hardware, software, installation facility, process design, training etc, and all specific to the industry in which the customer operated and down to the customer's business itself. When you're dealing with an uneducated market where you know infinitely more about the product than the customer it's an enormous relief to him that you're prepared to take total responsibility for his need. And, as IBM was keenly aware, he's willing to pay handsomely for it.

But an uneducated market doesn't stay that way forever and if part of your service is to educate the customer yourself, you have to plan for the day when the market no longer needs or wants the style of service that you offer. That proved particularly true in the case of the computer market whose product became (and is still increasingly becoming) ever more comprehensible and user-friendly. In the mid 1970s the point was reinforced with the coming of the new mini-computer which led the way for companies to do for themselves all the installation, software, training and support that they'd previously been paying good old IBM the proverbial arm and leg to do for them.

So what was the reaction of our marketing superhero? Well, with a philosophy of 'give the market what it wants', there was only one thing it could do. It dropped the peripheral added-value services and concentrated on selling machines. The market wanted boxes, so IBM moved boxes. Many corporations would have acted defensively to protect their product package and marketing style, but not IBM: it anticipated and moved with the market even to the destruction and replacement of its product and selling style. And you've got to admire the strategy, 'cos that's marketing.

Divestment

The title of this book is 'Going for Growth' and the assumption is that you're developing a corporate plan to enable your company to achieve this, but exactly what do you mean by growth – physical space occupied, number of staff, turnover? In all probability each of these will be implied but fundamentally you're in business to make profits and unless profits themselves are growing, achieving growth in anything else is a fairly pointless exercise. So what happens when you've got a subsidiary or division that is failing to contribute to profit or, worse, making losses and actually detracting from profit earned by other segments of the business?

First, there will always be some circumstances in which this state of affairs is tolerable. Most newly established businesses start by making losses and so long as those losses are budgeted and contained within manageable limits for a restricted period, there should be no long-term problem. More difficult is the situation where a business has been profitable but is no longer or has simply never achieved the profitability that was expected of it.

If you face this situation in a part of your own business there are two possible extremes of reaction that are equally inadvisable. Either you take the view that it has to be saved at all costs and concentrate on it to the detriment of your profitable activities or you decide to get rid of it at any cost. It is very often the size of parent business compared with problem subsidiary that determines towards which of these extremes you lean. The bigger the gap the more likely the parent is to want to get rid of the thorn in its corporate flesh as quickly as possible. It's all too easy to react to a problem by wanting it to go away rather than rolling up the shirt sleeves and solving it.

Whether it's possible to return the sick child to full health will depend on the cause of the illness. But one interesting fact widely ignored by divestors the world over is that if you're going to sell a business, there has to be somebody out there willing to buy it ... and people only buy businesses if they think they can run them at a profit. If they can put those assets to profitable use, how come you can't? Maybe you're concerned about the future of the market or your ability to reach it, but unless the purchaser is a fool he knows about the marketing problem and intends to solve it. What's stopping you from doing the same? Most corporate problems come down to management problems and if you're selling essentially because of management failure it's a problem the buyer intends to solve. What's stopping you from doing the same? The buyer is most likely to solve the problem by spending time on it, and you may be inclined to think that time is the one thing you haven't got. But is he going to spend the time himself or is he going to get someone else to do it? If it's the latter, what's stopping you from doing the same? All this is intended to amount to one thought-provoking point: while there may ultimately be good reasons for disposing of the business, most of the reasons for which people part with unprofitable activities are ill-considered and in many cases plainly wrong.

There is, however, another side to the coin, and in some circumstances divestment can be the right move. For example, you may have grown a business to a point where the only way forward is a quantum leap which requires a substantial cash investment. You may not have access to those funds, or if you do you may have potentially better uses for them elsewhere in the business. Alternatively, you may be approached by a purchaser who can genuinely make better use of your business than you can by combining your activities with what he's already doing. Under such circumstances it's not uncommon for a prospective purchaser to offer a capital sum in excess of what you may feel the business to be worth with regard to the profits it's currently generating. The temptation is, of course, to grab the cash and run because you naturally look at what the business is worth to you. But just stop long enough to look at what it's worth to the buyer and the picture changes somewhat. Combined with his own assets, the profit stream he's going to generate from your business may be much higher than you're currently able to achieve; ask yourself how good the price looks in that context. If you're one of many businesses doing what you do, you may be in a competitive situation and that could tend to force the price down, but if you're unique you're in an environment that's highly susceptible to negotiation. And don't think you need to take a single cash sum and stand back to watch the buyer make millions out of your business. How about a share of increased profitability over the next year or two? Or how about selling only a part of the business so that you benefit from the increased profitability that the buyer is intending to generate? The possible variations are virtually without limit. The only problem is stopping yourself grabbing the cash for long enough to think about and act on some of them.

There is another reason commonly voiced for divestment, particularly among the larger international conglomerates and particularly during periods of economic recession. It usually sounds something like this: 'It no longer fits in with our corporate objective' or 'We would prefer to concentrate on our main areas of activity and dispose of peripheral businesses.' Where a large group has acquired a small group that has incompatible subsidiaries there may be grounds for adopting this kind of strategy. But sadly, the conglomerates who are now preaching the philosophy of divestment most loudly are the very same ones that 20 years ago shouted the virtues of acquisition and diversification from the rooftops. If ever there was an example of the breakdown in strategic planning, this is it.

Chapters 7 and 8 look at the potential advantages of

diversification and acquisition of other businesses. These strategies will be right for some businesses and divestment right for others. Indeed, over a period of time, both approaches may be right but ultimately the only right strategy is the one that results in sustainable increased profitability for your business. The acquisition made for strategic reasons five years ago is unlikely to require disposal for the same strategic reasons now.

One of the most interesting phenomena to result from the spate of conglomerate divestment in the mid-1980s has been the management buyout where the managers of a given division buy the business from the group. A large number of management groups have done extremely well out of the process, nearly always at the expense of the parent company – many of them perfect examples of one-sided deals where the divestment was too small for the parent to bother negotiating seriously.

Take the example of one of the earlier buyouts that took place back in 1982. UK Company Limited was a small subsidiary of a US oil giant that was looking to dispose of peripheral interests in Europe. The UK management team got wind of the disposal and approached a merchant bank for assistance. The team and the bank together structured a proposal to the parent company who, as it turned out, could hardly be bothered to take notice of its tiny (£2½ million) subsidiary. Because of the insignificance of the UK group to the parent's balance sheet, the management team was able to argue effectively for a very low price based on such factors as tax and bad debt provisions that were very unlikely ever to be used. The final result was an acquisition of a profitable company for very little more than net asset worth. The managers promptly floated the company at a healthy premium and became wealthy men overnight – all at the effective expense of the US parent who was simply glad to be rid of a nuisance. This may or may not have been an acceptable divestment in strategic terms but what was and still is clear is that the parent was too constrained by numbers on the balance sheet to think the strategic issues through clearly and consider the alternatives, which might have ranged from floating the subsidiary off itself to putting in a new chief executive. The moral of the story is that, however big or small you are, think carefully before disposing of a business to *anyone* willing to buy it: it will almost always be worth more to him than he's willing to pay; it may also be worth more to you.

Assuming then that you're not just going to take the easy way out and simply sell, what are the alternatives for the ailing subsidiary? A number of courses of action are likely to be open to you but a good place to start is by assessing what the prospective purchaser might have been expected to do with it. You may be able to determine this from his track record, particularly if he has a trail of acquisitions behind him. If he's an asset stripper, look closely at the market value of your assets. No one's suggesting you should destroy your business and throw the workforce on the streets just to gain the benefits of selling the assets. But if, for example, there's development value in your freehold site, consider the possibility of selling the site itself and running the business from another location. If your intended purchaser is a manager, look closely at whether you're getting all you should out of your management team. If you can't identify the problem get the good old management consultant in again to find out what's wrong and put it right. And if at the end of all this you're still determined to sell up, the minimum that you should have achieved is the identification of arguments to force the price up.

One final point: if you do get into negotiations for sale, don't do it on your own. If the buyer's any good at all he'll have professional advice on his side. Get it on yours as well and you stand a much better chance of doing well out of the deal. If your professional adviser can't cover his own costs in negotiations, you've got the wrong person advising you.

Summary

This and the previous chapter have assumed that whichever of the main routes of corporate strategy you decide to go for, generic growth is likely to play a large part in the achievement of your targets. This chapter has highlighted three specific matters that are worthy of attention in consideration of growth of existing activities.

1. *Contribution.* To make accounting work positively for you rather than using it simply to keep score, adopt a contribution and variable cost approach to monthly management accounting. Analysing your performance in relation to fixed and variable costs helps you to appreciate the action you need to take to maximise profitability in a range of circumstances.
2. *Marketing.* The purpose of marketing is to create the right environment in the market-place for the sale of your products. You must create in the mind of the buyer an awareness of his

need for the product, the attractions of you as a supplier and your products above all others on the market. The best way to do that is not *necessarily* to do what everyone else in the market is doing. If the marketing process is not producing the results, find out why and take positive action.

3. *Divestment.* The line of least resistance when dealing with an unprofitable business is to sell it, but other than in a limited range of specific circumstances it is unlikely to be the most profitable response. Find out what the proposed buyer intends to do with the business and examine the possibility of doing the same before you sell.

Chapter 7
Diversification

It has already been argued that in most cases the primary route forward is likely to be through growth in the existing level of activities that your business undertakes. But for a whole host of reasons, this may not give you the growth that you've decided, at the strategic level, to aim for over the next few years. That means it's decision time again. If you can't expand by this route, there are two principal alternatives open to you: buy out someone who's already operating in the same field or do something else yourself (which may also mean continuing the existing business on an increased scale but at a new location).

There may be a natural attraction in buying out another business that's up and running but there are pitfalls too and Chapter 8 looks at the pros and cons in detail. The purpose of this chapter is to help you look at the possibility of diversifying your business as the best step forward to achieving the desired level of growth.

Before thinking further about either acquisition or diversification as growth strategies, there's one fundamental rule to observe:

> Acquisition and diversification must not be undertaken as defensive or negative measures because you are unhappy with some aspect of the way you are conducting your present business. As tools for gaining growth they will only work if undertaken as part of a positive, aggressive strategy.

If something within the existing business is preventing you from achieving the growth you could otherwise expect, you must put it right before attempting to diversify. In any case, you should have picked it up during the initial process of establishing your current business position. Don't underestimate the additional strain that diversification will put on your existing business. If you try to

107

superimpose that strain on an already weak structure it's going to crack. Resolve the internal problems first and you'll be able to go on to successful diversification – if indeed that is the best way forward for your company. When considering the applicability of the concept to your unique circumstances, bear one point in mind: some diversification strategies should really carry a government health warning along the following lines:

Ill considered diversification strategy can seriously damage your corporate health.

Not because diversification is dangerous *per se* but rather because when it is undertaken, it's very often for the wrong reasons or done in the wrong way. Let's start by considering some of the valid reasons why you may want to go for it in the first place.

Why diversify?

1. The one-product company may face problems

Almost every small business starts life as a one-product company. You establish yourself as a manufacturer of widgets, or proprietor of a restaurant or whatever it happens to be and, of course, may stay happily at that level for evermore. But if it's your intention to grow there can be dangers in remaining a one-product business. First, you're exposed to the possibility of someone much larger and with much more clout setting up very close by and competing. If it comes to a real fight and he's capable of sustaining the battle for longer than you are, you're in trouble. Second, business is a heartless environment and the market a fickle place. Businessmen tend to assume that there's always going to be a buyer for their product because there always has been, but if you're in an industry that is potentially susceptible to technological change or subject to the dictates of fashion, take no comfort from the argument; the market or technology can leave you high and dry overnight. Third, if you're ever likely to be looking for a financier to put equity capital into your business, don't go looking while you are a one-product company. For all the reasons noted above (and also because of pure prejudice) financiers don't like the one-product company and unless your business is very unusual they're not likely to take a fancy to you.

Look at a couple of examples of how businesses have fared in this context. X Limited was a newly formed company established for the purpose of developing a safe deposit centre in a wealthy area of south London. The proprietors had no experience in the field but had seen others making money doing much the same sort of thing. The problem was that they had no funds of their own to back the project. They approached several financial institutions for money but received broadly the same answer at each port of call. Inexperience, lack of personal funding and the one-product, one-location concept ensured that the project never got off the ground.

By contrast, take the example of the computer company in west London mentioned in Chapter 5. That company had problems which took some time to resolve but it was making enough impact in its area to come to the notice of a much larger predator, who approached the proprietors with a view to buying them out. When the proposal was declined the suitor became quite aggressive, threatening intense local competition, and pointed out that, given the small one-product status, survival could be in question. While for other reasons the immediate threat receded, the proprietors took the hint and diversified into other items – facsimile machines and car telephones initially – and other locations thereafter. The result? The problem never repeated itself and all the new areas of activity proved to be profitable (although it needs to be said that these changes were tactical responses to an outside influence and not part of a strategic plan).

2. Your present market may not have the capacity to absorb your growth intentions

It all depends on how far forward you want your strategy to take you and how fast you want to go. If you're a relatively small manufacturer of a nationally consumed product then the chances are that the market can absorb any rate of growth you can cope with internally (unless you are dealing with a very small segment of a big market, in which case you could need extra capacity). But if the emphasis of your product is exclusive or the primary market you address is small relative to your own size, you may face a difficulty. The latter may apply, for example, to a small local retailer who, in addition, may face the constraint of physical capacity in his existing location.

Take, as a more specific example, the case of a manufacturer of a very exclusive, very limited range of kitchens. The company had grown for a number of years at a rate far in excess of the growth of the market itself. Further growth was both desired and anticipated, but because the product was sold largely on its exclusivity the proprietors were wary of the dangers of over-penetrating the market. There were two main tenets to the plan: first, a cautious move into exporting, thus allowing the company to address new markets; second, the opening of direct retail outlets offering the company the retail profits on their product that previously went to other companies. Particular care was taken to site retail outlets so as to avoid direct competition with retailers who already carried the product.

3. Diversifying into complementary products may allow you to sell more of your existing range

Although diversification can mean launching out into a completely different area of activity from anything you've done before, it doesn't have to. At its simplest it can mean simply putting a new product into an existing range. Get that product right and it can do wonders for the sales of your existing business. Just to finish the story about the kitchen company, it didn't stop at export and retail. To the basic product of kitchen units it went on to add appliances (having previously supplied other people's), wall tiles and lighting. Despite fears that it was reaching full capacity in the UK market, its home sales continued to rise at a gratifying rate. Moral: if there's a product that customers normally buy in conjunction with your own, ask yourself why you're not supplying it. Nine times out of ten you could be, and it could do wonders for sales of your existing range. We all have a natural disinclination to waste time and one-stop shopping is a very attractive concept. Why aren't you providing it?

4. Markets move in cycles

Cycles can be either very good or very bad for your business. Anyone in the toy industry, the tourist industry or the building industry will tell you that markets move in cycles. Most other markets do the same but may not be as clearly perceived to do so. If cyclical activity is a problem in your business, look into the possibility of diversifying into another market that moves on a different cycle, but be careful how you go about it.

A small subcontracting firm in the building industry perceived that it faced this problem and over a period of time considered the possibility of undertaking other activities. (It's only fair to mention that these other activities were considered as profitable opportunities in themselves, not just defensively for counter-cyclical purposes.) In due course it set up its own house building division and a precision tool machine shop as well. Misfortune struck when the MD died and his sons took over the running of the business. At just the time when most attention should have been devoted to the running of the new activities, weakness hit the core business. From that time on the company went downhill until it eventually ended in the hands of the liquidator some ten years later. A sad story but one of countless examples of not getting diversification right. That's why, having decided that it offers a sensible opportunity for contributing towards the achievement of the corporate goal, giving effect to the diversification properly is crucially important.

How to diversify

It all depends on your circumstances and what you're trying to achieve. As already stated, the term diversification can cover anything from putting new products on the shelves, through setting up an extra outlet, to launching out into completely new territory. The approaches that you need to take will depend on exactly where within this spectrum you fall, and inevitably each situation is unique. However, there are a number of ground rules that you need to observe and the first of these has already been referred to.

1. Never diversify if there's something fundamentally wrong with the existing business

When there is a problem with your present operation it's tempting to look at doing something else, either to help you forget the problem or in a genuine attempt to inject some stability into the situation through a completely new avenue. However, do remember that it's highly unlikely that fundamental problems will resolve themselves without assistance and that usually means from you, the MD. If you're simply not available because you're concentrating on a new product or location or venture, the wound is likely to fester.

By contrast, if the organisation that you're building on to is strong and virtually capable of running itself, you have a stable base on which to build a new activity. Anything new, by virtue of the fact that it is new, takes a disproportionate amount of time and attention and will face more than its fair share of problems. So get the existing base stable and then launch out into new activities, or Murphy's law will dictate that just when you need to concentrate most on the new venture, trouble at t'mill will demand your attention.

2. Select the form of diversification at a strategic level before you look for specific opportunities

If you have a business that's up and running, by definition you've proved yourself to be a businessman already. Out there in the big wide world are a million and one opportunities for you to make a profit, and having decided to go for diversification the temptation may just be to jump at the first one that happens along. While it may be potentially profitable, it may not be right for you and your existing activities. You must think as carefully about each step along the route to expansion as you thought about launching out into business on your own in the first place. That decision was based on careful thought about your own skills, market opportunity, location and a whole host of other considerations it's not appropriate to cover here. Don't let the decision to diversify be any less carefully considered and let that consideration be first at the strategic level before you look for specific opportunities. Establish clearly in your own mind the reasons why you're looking for diversification and then look for situations that will meet the need. The requirements of an expansionist greengrocer who has hit capacity in one location will be different from the West Country hotelier who needs something to reduce his overdraft in the off-season. The former will be looking for another location in another town to exploit his successful formula; the latter may target the conference market to fill his empty rooms from November to March. There is no apparent need for either to diversify into activities counter-cyclical to the whole of their markets and of which they have no knowledge. (However, each must bear in mind that while the product area is not new to him, the new market segment addressed is.)

If the point hasn't become obvious already, let it be clearly stated: diversification into activities of which you have no knowledge is one of the most dangerous steps that a small business can take. There's little in business that's safe, but it's potentially one of the least safe steps of all. So if you're thinking of doing it in the first place, do it for the right reasons and do as much as you can to minimise the risk. Strategically, it's a step that should only be considered in a limited range of circumstances, for example:

- when your status as a one-product company is becoming a problem;
- when there are no more opportunities for growth through other media.

To these conditions you may be inclined to add one more:

- when an opportunity is presented which is too good to miss

and that has to be the most dangerous form of diversification known to man. The main caveat applicable to any diversification is fundamental here:

3. If you don't have access to the required expertise, don't do it

The reason that you were successful in the establishment of your own business was because you had the relevant expertise. Don't be tempted to take on something else unless the same level of expertise is available in the new activity, at least not if you're considering a completely new business or a new activity that is large in comparison with your present business base. If you're looking at the possibility of a new location, choose it with the same care as you selected your present business base. If you're introducing a new product or service that relies on essentially the same expertise as you applied last time round, investigate the feasibility of the idea with the same degree of care as you did previously. When you first went into business and funds were limited you knew you couldn't afford to make a loss. Just because you now have a profit stream to rely on you should not be prepared to fund a start-up loss in the new project for any longer than necessary.

However, don't be deceived into thinking that the expertise for a new venture has to come from yourself or your management. If you need to undertake a new project and don't have the necessary expertise, buy it. The kitchen manufacturers referred to on p. 109 knew that their expertise lay in manufacturing and selling kitchens. When the time came to move into retailing and export they located and bought in the necessary expertise to cope with the areas of activity in which their expertise was lacking. Or take the example of a group of managers who bought out their company in the leisure industry. On one of their larger entertainment sites they wanted to build a hotel. No one on the board had the necessary experience, so initially industry consultants were called in to assess the feasibility of the concept. In addition it happened that, by pure coincidence, some committed and trusted employees of the company were already experienced in the hotel business. Once the feasibility of the project was established, it only remained for a manager to be located and employed.

4. Minimise the risk

Being in business is all about taking risks but those risks must be assessed, controlled and minimised. If you don't do so you're not in business, you're merely a gambler. The potential reward has to be attractive in comparison with the risk you're taking or there's no point in undertaking the project. One way to minimise risk once the project is under way is to make sure that you have the necessary expertise on hand to make it work. You can also take a number of measures long before you get to the total commitment stage to ensure you're doing it right. Always consider test marketing a new product before committing yourself to large orders or production runs. It is by no means unknown for even the most respected experts to gauge market reaction totally wrongly, and if you're going to be wrong, be wrong small first. Having gone through the testing stage and confirmed everything looks OK, do you really have to tool up for large production runs straight off? Consider the possibility of subcontracting manufacture until sales hit the level where you know you've got it right.

Take the example of a small firm that produced bolt-on parts for cabin cruisers. The product was looked on favourably by all who examined it at the design stage. Encouraged, the directors put together a business plan to look for funding to go into production. After much disappointment money was found, but only on the basis that production was subcontracted thus saving the cost of setting up a production facility. As it turned out, wisdom lay with the financiers. There was too much industry resistance and the product did not succeed – but that's business.

5. Integrate the new activity into your organisational structure as soon as possible

In Chapter 2 when we were establishing where your business is now, the point was made that to get the business running smoothly you have to get the operational structure and the lines of responsibility right. If your current business has grown in something of a haphazard manner, you've probably had to face the need to restructure at some point. Assuming that's been done, now that you're considering diversification you're looking at an opportunity to get the structure right from the start. Set up the new venture correctly now and you won't face all the problems of doing it in five years' time when custom, practice and people's opinions and self-esteem will hamper your every move.

In addition to setting it up right, there are good reasons to integrate the new area of business with your existing activities as soon as possible. The longer you try to run the new venture as a separate business, the more likely it is that rivalry will grow up between the staff of the new and the staff of the old. The quicker you integrate it, the sooner you'll be able to give responsibility for its running to others in the organisation and concentrate elsewhere yourself. The sooner integration is achieved, the less chance there will be of key employees walking out, and the less serious such a loss will be.

Timing and scale

Timing diversification can be crucial and like everything else in business it needs to be planned from the strategic level downwards. In this case you have two different perspectives from which you must take the strategic view: that of your current activities and that of the area into which you are about to move. The temptation that most entrepreneurs find difficult to resist is rushing into something that looks good, and there are always good reasons why the opportunity needs to be taken yesterday. But bear in mind the seriousness of the step; you're considering something that is intended to be a long-term contributor to the success and growth of your business. If it's the kind of chance that has to be taken now or not at all, it's probably not got the characteristics that you're looking for anyway. To rush into something that has to be done now denies you the ability to take a strategic approach to growth, and growth without strategy is likely to be growth without stability. Anyway, life's rich experience always seems to offer another opportunity a little further down the road.

Having taken the strategic decision on the form of diversification that you want to go for, what next? Because it's diversification and not acquisition that you're looking at, at this stage it should be possible to devote adequate time to investigation and implementation without the fear of final deadlines looming up on you, ie you should be able to move at a gentle enough pace to make sure that you're getting it right at each stage. Having arrived at the strategic decision to diversify, go on to investigate at length each of the possibilities open to you. Because the product or service that you plan to introduce is new, you'll obviously need to spend a considerable amount of time investigating the market potential, establishing whether your existing customers are likely to buy and targeting new customers who can be approached. Equally, you'll need to investigate sources of supply and be satisfied that they won't dry up shortly after you launch out into new areas.

After undertaking investigations into the concept of each diversification opportunity open, you then face possibly the hardest decision in the process – which of the several possibilities investigated will you go for? It's a decision that you will only be able to take in the light of your requirements (which possibility offers the best hope of achieving the aims of your diversification strategy) and the chances of success (which of the possibilities is most likely to be successfully implemented). But having arrived at the decision, the key to successful execution is (yet again) adequate planning. Treat planning at this stage as a completely separate exercise from the strategic process you have undergone to get this far. You've planned at the highest strategic level for the achievement of an overall corporate objective. You're now planning for the successful implementation of a project, and there's nothing to be gained by running the two together. The objective of the exercise is now to get the new product introduced, or the new retail division up and running. Plan with reference to the objective and you stand the best chance of achieving it.

As for time-scale, it's difficult to say. Much will depend on the scale of the project both in absolute terms and relative to the size of your existing business. The temptation is to think that because you're taking the time to plan, the process will take longer. However, experience will prove time and again that from start to finish the planned process is likely to take less time and be more successful than the unplanned equivalent.

Finally, as far as scale is concerned, the only point that can usefully be made should be fairly obvious: it's not generally a good idea to take on something very large in comparison with your existing level of operations. The larger and more expensive the project, the greater the risk and the higher the cost of failure. However, the world is not an ideal place and in many cases growth has to be stepped rather than gradual. Clearly, business is all about calculated risks and if you're not a risk taker you shouldn't be in business at all. The only maxim that can be applied, therefore, is: the bigger the risk you're taking the more care you must apply in getting it right. The rewards of a big risk may look great, but the consequences of failure can be disastrous.

Summary

1. Simply doing more of what you do now may not be the best or even an available route to growth. If circumstances dictate that it's not the way forward for you, growth by diversification may be a possiblity. However, you can't use diversification to solve problems within the existing business. Any deficiencies that are there are more likely to become a greater problem when you impose the additional strain that diversification will bring.

2. Why should you diversify?
   - because it offers a solution to some of the problems of a one-product company;
   - because the market you presently address may not offer the capacity to allow you to grow at the rate you would like;
   - because diversified products may help to sell items already in the range;
   - because diversification may offset some of the problems of a cyclical business.

3. How should you diversify?
   - by first ensuring the current business is sufficiently stable to take the strain;
   - by selecting the route for diversification strategically before taking practical steps;
   - by gaining access to the expertise required for the new area of activity;
   - by approaching diversification in a manner which minimises the risk;
   - by integrating the new area of activity into your existing structure as quickly as possible.

4. Timing and scale of activities:
   - timing is crucial – do not be rushed into moving before you're ready and get it right at the strategic level first;
   - investigate the alternative possibilities properly, with emphasis on market potential;

117

- plan execution of your selected route properly;
- minimise the risk by keeping the scale of activities low.

Chapter 8
Acquisition

It has been argued through much of this text that the principal route forward for most companies will be generic growth – doing more of what you do now. In the event that this is not feasible for some reason (see for example Appendix 1), the first resort should be to consider thoroughly the overall strategic objectives which have been established and how, in the absence of adequate generic growth, these might be best served. Thereafter, the preferable route will normally be diversification on a scale that does not risk the main operation unduly. Only if there are real barriers to achieving the objectives by diversification should the possibility of acquisition be considered, since it will normally be a costlier route than the former, requiring more substantial capital outlay.

There is, however, one other significant reason why you may wish to consider acquisition: because an unexpected opportunity presents itself to you. If you're in this category, weigh up very carefully whether the opportunity is really all you believe it to be and make sure that you're not getting caught up in the excitement of the moment. Further, assess equally carefully whether the chance you are being offered takes you closer to your defined objectives, and before you commit yourself to an unexpected opportunity think about whether it's the kind of chance you would have wanted had you been looking for ways forward. Finally, if it's one of those once-in-a-lifetime, too-good-to-be-missed, now-or-never chances, unless you're *very* sure and you've taken objective advice, walk away from it, because it's almost certain that you have it out of perspective.

However, if after all the above you're still taking a reasoned and serious look at the possibility of acquiring another business, there are a number of questions which you will need to address, not the least of which is:

Why acquire another business?

Assuming that the arguments ring true for diversification being preferable to acquisition, there has to be a reason for going on the acquisition trail at all. The number of possible reasons at the strategic level are, in fact, fairly limited:

1. Time
One of the disadvantages of growing a new business from nothing is that it takes time to get it going. Usually you're looking at years rather than months to make a new venture a success and that kind of time you may simply not have. To take the acquisition route for this reason is effectively to place a high monetary value on the time-scale for achieving your strategic objectives. But if time is very much of the essence, acquisition may be a feasible alternative to doing it the harder and less expensive way.

2. Expertise
If you firmly believe that you're a manufacturer of left-handed widgets and all your experience lies in that product and no more, you can use acquisition as a strategy to buy in established team expertise in right-handed widgets. Of course, if you need only one person who knows the right-handed market, you're better off buying him in, but if you need a team of experienced people all of whom will have slightly different expertise, acquisition of a business already producing right-handed widgets could be one way of getting the bodies on board. However, one word of warning is appropriate: if it's the people that you're after, bear in mind that a change of ownership can often be the cause of a mass exodus by the staff. So if the people are the business, make sure that they're tied in to ensure you don't lose them. (See page 134 for details of ways in which they can be locked into the business.)

3. An introduction into a market
It may be the case that you're world famous as a producer of left-handed widgets, but when the market looks right for right-handed widgets yours would be the last name that anyone would think of. Overcoming this kind of customer inertia by marketing alone can be a laborious task, particularly if there are established and respected names in the new market already. If your entry into a market could be forestalled because of this and because of customer resistance, buying an established name with a standing

reputation can be a solution. However, before you follow this route, make sure that the name you're going to buy really is synonymous with the image you want to project in the marketplace.

4. A client list

For similar reasons to those outlined in 3 above, it can be difficult to get started in a business which is heavily dependent on large established client lists. Consequently, it may be the case that the only way into this kind of market is to buy in, and that means the acquisition of someone else's business. Take, for example, Mr P, an experienced and established salesman of unit trust based insurance schemes. His company, the subsidiary of a large financial conglomerate, worked from a client list of over 40,000 names. Mr P wanted to establish his own business but to build up a client list of similar proportions would have taken several man-years' work. Accordingly, Mr P and his professional advisers approached the board of the parent company who, for various reasons, were willing to allow a buyout.

5. Assets

By acquiring a business, it may be possible to gain access to assets at an attractive price or, possibly, to items which are not available elsewhere. The case study quoted in Appendix 1 illustrates the point. Footloose Limited was looking for an opportunity to grow at a faster than market rate. When Cavalier Limited came on the market, it offered the company an avenue into a segment of the market which they had not previously been able to address. Further, it offered them access to plant and machinery otherwise only available new at an astronomical price. Because the sale price of Cavalier was set with reference to income stream not asset base, the plant was effectively acquired at a knock-down price.

Locating potential acquisitions

Locating possible acquisitions starts once again at the strategic level. Depending on what you are and what you do, location could be largely irrelevant or crucially important. Your examination of where your business is now should have established clearly the importance of physical location to your present business. But when you go on the acquisition trail, remember that by having an additional business unit, you may be fundamentally changing the nature of your whole operation. Consider whether location will be important in the new environment and choose your way forward carefully. Having done so, targeting potential acquisitions is, first and foremost, a matter of identifying those features which will serve your corporate goals best. Translate your strategy into a list of identifiable requirements and you will have a profile for your ideal acquisition. Then, and only then, will you be in a position to seek out a target, because only then will you be in a position to assess properly the extent to which a potential target measures up to the requirements of your strategic objectives.

At this point, you are probably the best person to know how to locate possible targets, without any help from the corporate strategists! There are likely to be two primary areas of possibility though. Either because of your knowledge of your industry you will have an idea of which companies are feasible acquisitions, or certain businesses will be on the market already. If you're looking at cases of the former, the next stage is a matter of familiarising yourself with your target as much as possible, finding its strengths and weaknesses and determining its ownership. Then you need to make your approach to whoever in the target company is most suitable – and that's the crucial point. You are, presumably, going to buy the shares and consequently, it's the principal shareholders who matter in the final event. But there may be someone else whose opinion will be listened to more than any other. He might be a board member, a professional adviser or the local vicar. Whoever it is, your most important task is to locate that person and understand what makes him tick. If you can establish what motivates him and what you can offer him, you're a long way down the road to a successful acquisition.

However, if you're dealing with the other category, the company that's already on the market, the whole concept is rather different. In this case, the owners have already decided to dispose of their interest and that leaves one question which dominates all others and must be answered before you go any further:

Why are they selling?

There are lots of good reasons for selling a business. The vendors may be reaching retirement age and have no one to whom they can hand the running of the business. If the vendor is a large conglomerate, the decision may have been taken to dispose of peripheral areas of activity to allow management more time to concentrate on the core business. Similarly, in smaller cases, the vendors may have more than one interest and wish to divest themselves of some to allow them time to concentrate on others. Any 'good' reason for sale should not be a problem to you as potential purchaser. However, there are two other categories of reason for disposal which should make you much more cautious about the possibility of buying:

1. The business is about to demand something in the foreseeable future which the vendor is not able or not inclined to give it.
2. There is something fundamentally wrong with the business which the vendor is either unable to identify or unable to correct.

In the former category, you're looking at factors such as the need to make substantial capital expenditure, undertake the development of new products because the present range is approaching the end of its life cycle or expected competitive activity etc. If you are looking at a possible acquisition which falls into this category, there are two questions that you really need to ask yourself before getting too involved. First, 'If I buy this business, will I face the same requirements that are being imposed on the vendor?' The answer will almost certainly be 'Yes', unless, for example, the requirement is for capital expenditure and you only want the company for its client list. Second, if the answer is 'Yes', ask yourself, 'Am I in a position to fulfil this requirement, if I buy the business?' Obviously, if the answer is 'No', then look elsewhere for your acquisition.

The second category, the 'fundamental problem', can be more difficult to deal with, not least because you're unlikely to persuade the vendor into admitting that there is a problem. No one selling an asset will go out of his way to draw deficiencies to the attention of potential purchasers. Take the example of a small butcher's shop in a dormitory town south of London. The shop changed hands recently. The purchaser asked to see accounts to back up the claim of £1,800 per week turnover that had been quoted. Mysteriously, accounts were not available because the vendor had 'several shops that were all accounted for centrally'. The purchaser had asked if the large cold store attached to the shop was in working order. 'It only needs switching on', was the reply. Needless to say, after the purchaser moved in, turnover turned out to be £1,200 per week at best and the switch to the cold store (itself a very expensive item) was not working. The purchaser's solicitor suggested that there might be a case for legal action but for some reason, the vendor proved difficult to find.

The point is illustrative of a general principle which must be applied to the acquisition of all business – you *must* have adequate information to allow you:

- to decide if you really want to buy at all;
- to establish a reasonable price to bid.

Only when you know what the business is about, warts and all, will you be in a position to decide what its problems are, whether you have the time and expertise available to solve them and whether buying is such a good idea after all. The question now arises as to how you can establish the real status of the business and that's where you have to turn to the knotty problem of:

Using professional advisers

When most people undertake a significant legal transaction, they employ the services of a solicitor, grit their teeth and accept that it's going to be expensive. Not unreasonably, they take the view that they'd like to be secure in the knowledge that they have actually ended up owning whatever it is they want to buy. However, for some incomprehensible reason, in the purchase of a business many fail to establish the quality of what they're buying by using investigators to examine the acquisition. You may not be able to find industry specialists in, say, butchers' shops but you can use reporting accountants or general business consultants to investigate intelligently most business acquisitions. Nobody pretends that it's cheap to do so, but it can be worthwhile from two points of view: first, it gives comfort that everything is what it seems; second, anything that you find out as a result of the investigation can be used as a bargaining tool to lever the price down.

Take the example of a merchant bank which set up a subsidiary to invest in commodity stockholding. It was advised that, for tax reasons, it ought to trade in the commodity as well and consequently went out looking for existing specialist shops. Having located a possible target in the form of a small chain of retail outlets, it was discovered that the vendors were actually quite a large conglomerate operation themselves and (surprise, surprise) were a little cagey about their reasons for selling. A preliminary price was agreed subject to investigation and investigating accountants put in to report. Suffice it to say that the report produced clearly identified a number of problem areas which were used to negotiate a price reduction in excess of 20 per cent which was more than adequate to reflect both the cost of rectifying the problems and the cost of the accountant's fee.

Establishing a price

If you've followed through the process logically so far, you will know clearly your reasons for wanting to acquire another business, you may have located and targeted a possible acquisition and established (if the business is already on the market) the vendor's reasons for selling. If you actually intend to press on and go through with a deal, the next requirement is to determine a price. Regardless of what a potential vendor wants for the business, there is one, and only one, way of establishing an acceptable price from your point of view and it involves answering clearly and logically (and on paper if necessary) the question: 'What is the business worth to me?'

When an item is offered for sale at a stated price, that price has a habit of assuming a somewhat mystical characteristic. If the transaction is to take place in an environment where negotiation is abnormal (such as retail shops), the price rarely, if ever, varies. The vendor may move it up and down to attract customers into the shop, but once they're in, the transaction will normally take place at the stated price or not at all. Similarly, if the environment is one in which negotiation is traditional (such as a second-hand car showroom), negotiation will take place based on the asking price. All this is perfectly natural and normal but from the point of view of the purchaser, consider who actually has the greatest influence over price. Clearly, the answer is not you, the purchaser, but the *vendor*. The reason that this normally happens is because it is the vendor who usually initiates the transaction. And how does he go about setting the price? Perhaps he may consider what the item is worth to him. More normally, he will set the price by reference to what he thinks you, the purchaser, will be prepared to pay.

The purpose of all this is to demonstrate that *minimising the price is all about taking the initiative* and there are two ways of doing it. If you're looking at a business already on the market, you must establish if possible how the price has been arrived at and demolish the philosophy on which it has been set. For example, if the vendor has fixed his price range by reference to underlying asset values, your job is to prove that the future income stream is the only valid basis for setting price and why that income stream will not be good. If price has been set with reference to a market norm the strategy must be to establish reasons why market norm is too high.

Where you're dealing with a business which is not already on the market, your initial task may be that much easier since the owner may have no clear idea of what the business is worth even to himself (and while the point is under consideration, be clearly aware that there is no 'fair' price for any business since each is a unique organism with an infinitely variable range of characteristics – there is only a price which a vendor is prepared to accept and a purchaser prepared to pay). Where the owner has not considered the possible range of values of his business, you immediately have the upper hand. Suggest the possibility of a sale, suggest a value based on reasoned argument and negotiation will tend to start at that point. Had you approached the owner by asking him to suggest a price, he might have indicated a much higher range – most owners have an inflated view of the value of their asset until someone else deflates it for them! Theoretically, you also run the risk of setting a price range higher than the owner would have done, but avoiding that is largely a matter of doing your homework properly and establishing what his price range is likely to be.

Here it becomes crucial to have a reasoned answer to the question originally raised – 'What is the business worth to me?' – because at this point you're going into negotiations. It's a curious feature of human nature that when people get into negotiations or auctions they seem to end up giving away more than they intended to. To avoid doing so, you must have a clear idea of how much you are willing to go to and that in turn must be based on the plans you have for the business. Get things wrong at this stage and you could end up buying a business which will never turn in a profit which is adequate in light of the purchase price you pay.

There are a number of standard approaches to valuing a business and it's up to you to decide which is applicable to what you have in mind. Throughout the process remember, though, that what you are doing is not establishing a 'fair' price but one which reflects the value of the business to you in light of your own and the business's unique circumstances. Normally, if your intention is to continue running the business in more or less its present form, your valuation will tend to be based on the current income stream. Thus, the maximum price you are prepared to pay will be based on a multiple of current turnover, gross profitability or net profitability. Alternatively, you may intend to split up the assets of the business (say to sell a valuable lease and run the trade from your own current location). In this case, you would place a value on the business which also reflected the price you might expect to get for the lease.

Whichever way you do it, you are out to establish the maximum which you will be willing to pay once you get into negotiations, assuming the facts of the matter are as you currently perceive them. Of course, during the process of negotiation facts may come to light which influence your view of your maximum figure but these can only be taken into account as they arise.

Assuming you have established a maximum figure, the next step is to establish what the vendor might be prepared to accept and then, finally, at what price you ought to make your first pitch. As far as the former point is concerned, to do the job properly, you should go through the same process from the vendor's point of view as you have just been through from your own. Hopefully, there will be an area of overlap where his minimum price (or what you anticipate it to be) is lower than your maximum. If not, and if you've put yourself correctly in his shoes, expect difficult negotiations. When tempted to go too far, regularly reconsider the logic behind your own maximum price. Unless features come to light during the negotiation process which you had not previously considered, you have no reason to move from your position.

Finally, then, where do you start the ball rolling? Your first pitch must not be so low as to destroy your credibility as a serious bidder, yet it must be low enough to give you maximum flexibility in the negotiations. In addition, it must itself have logic as a sensible bid or you will immediately lose ground to the other side. It's not possible to state either a figure or a percentage of your maximum since every case will vary. Just bear in mind what you're trying to achieve and set your first shot accordingly.

There is one other point which needs to be made at this stage. Never negotiate on your own. The other party is unlikely to be doing so and having a two-pronged approach offers enormous benefits. Negotiations can become long and protracted and apart from anything else, it can be extremely tiring to hold your end up single-handed. In addition, the point in the process will come where the other side puts a case for which you can see no immediate answer. At that stage, the danger is that you go on the defensive and from there on you go downhill all the way. Having someone else there who is not leading the negotiations means another point of view and another brain to think of counter-arguments when you yourself slip up.

If all this sounds a little technical, there's one obvious (if potentially expensive) solution: call in the professionals. Once again, don't let the cost speak louder than the difference between success and expensive failure if something is important to you. Ultimately, it can be necessary to walk away, either because doing so is a useful tactic or because you and the vendor cannot see eye to eye. If you've got your approach to maximum price right and the vendor won't move into your ball park, don't be afraid to let it go. We all think losing a deal is the end of the world at the time but, without fail, there is always another one around the corner, and it could be better than the one you're looking at right now.

Financing the acquisition

By the time you get to the point of agreeing to buy the business in principle, you clearly have to be very confident of what you're doing. You will have established that you're buying the right business at the right price at the right time and you should have a clear idea of what you intend to do with it. By now, you will also have given thought to how the purchase is to be financed.

If the intention is to make the acquisition entirely out of your own resources, your only problem is to ensure that you retain adequate funds within your existing business to avoid cash flow problems. But if you're looking for funding from outside, the matter can quickly become very complex indeed.

During the first half of the 1980s, the market for funds for business became increasingly complicated and sophisticated, which, from the point of view of the seeker of funds can have both advantages and disadvantages. In addition, at the time of writing, money for business is easily available for good quality projects at the right price. Markets are fickle places, however, and there is no guarantee that such a positive environment has a long-term future, but while it persists the potential buyer of funds is at an advantage so long as he gets the quality of his proposition right. On the other hand, as suppliers of funds jostle with each other for a better competitive edge, the complexity of the product on offer increases, which serves to make the whole concept more confusing for the buyer. If the circumstances demand it, you can obtain funds which vary from the humble overdraft at one end of the scale through loans (of various terms and at fixed or variable rates of interest or a combination of both) to equity (redeemable, preferential, preferred or ordinary) and on to even weirder and more wonderful systems involving such things as joint ventures and levies on turnover.

If such a list sounds like a foreign language, do the sensible thing and seek professional help, but before doing so, it's possible to cut straight through all the complexities and, at least in the first instance, simplify the matter enormously. When it comes down to it, there are really only two main categories of funding which you have to consider, whether you're looking for money for a business purchase or for any other business use. On the one hand, there's the loan type, where you pay back what you borrow over some period and you pay a rate of interest for the privilege of borrowing. On the other hand, there is equity funding, whose overriding characteristic is that the supplier takes a (probably) permanent stake in the ownership of the business. Equity funding may also involve partial repayment of the funds and some rate of return. That's where the matter becomes very complex so that it can be difficult to decide how good a deal you're being offered. However, before you get as far as worrying about such matters, you need to decide which basic category of funding you're going to need, the loan type or the equity type.

Normally, the best advice is if your proposition is capable of being funded by way of loan type finance go this route rather than seek equity, for two reasons. First, loan finance is usually quicker, easier and cheaper to raise. Secondly, it has the overwhelming advantage that once you have paid it back you own the whole of your business as no one else has taken a permanent stake in it. In addition, it must be borne in mind that equity is a finite resource; you can only sell it once. If you're currently looking at a need which could be financed either by borrowing or by equity, it's usually best to go the loan route because one day you may be looking at a requirement which can only be financed by equity. If you've already sold as much as you want to part with, you have an unnecessary problem on your hands.

However, the question inevitably arises as to why people raise equity if loans are a better route. The first answer is normally that loan funding is not possible in certain circumstances. In addition to wanting interest on a loan, the provider of the money (and it's usually a banker of some description) will obviously be looking for some form of security – the confidence that he is going to get his money back. Now, you may have all the confidence in the world that your project will produce the most amazing returns but unless you can give your backer some acceptable security to hang his loan on, he's likely to walk away from the deal. In addition, bankers have a clear order of preference as to which type of asset they like to use as security. Property is very popular (presumably because it has gone up in value for as long as anyone can remember), and typically, you'll find you can borrow between two-thirds and three-quarters of its value from most bankers. Good quality debtors are usually acceptable and bankers will normally lend perhaps 50 or 60 per cent of the book value so long as the debt hasn't been outstanding too long. Stock is not usually very popular among bankers but you might be able to borrow a small proportion of its value if you twist someone's arm.

Take an example to illustrate what may be possible. Assume that you've negotiated to buy an engineering business for £500,000 on the basis of the pre-tax profit it has made over the last three years. The profit figures have been:

Current Year £000	Last Year £000	Previous Year £000
150	140	130

You've targeted the business because you feel that you could exploit opportunities not open to the present proprietor but open to you. The balance sheet of the business is summarised as:

	£000	£000	£000	
Freehold property			100	(Market value £125,000)
Debtors		375		
Stock		50		
		425		
Overdraft	100			
Trade creditors	220	(320)	105	
			205	

There are a number of approaches you could take to finance the purchase, but assuming that you want to minimise the amount of cash which you need to part with personally, you would be best advised to consider first how much you could borrow against the assets of the business. A reasonable rule of thumb might give you the following:

		£000
Freehold at market value × ⅔		83
Debtors	× 60%	225
Stock	× 10%	5
		313
Less: Current overdraft facility		(100)
Borrowing capacity		213

To convince a banker to lend you this sort of sum you will have to put up a convincing case, because in addition to wanting good security, he needs to know you're able to pay the money back and are able to bear the interest payments. Interest at (say) 12 per cent will cost you £25,000 in the first year and if you borrow the whole sum over ten years, you'll need to pay a bank a further £22,000 per year as well. The interest will come out of profit before tax but the capital repayments come out of profit after tax. So, if you maintain profitability at the existing level, you'll need to take the following into account:

	£000
Profit before interest	150
Less interest	(25)
Profit before tax	125
Tax at (say) 35%	(44)
Profit after tax	81
Loan repayment	(22)
Remaining	59

So in order to borrow under half of what you need to buy the business, you've already reduced pre-tax profit of £150,000 to post-tax profits available for reinvestment/withdrawal to £59,000 and you still have £287,000 to raise!

Raising the rest of the finance may or may not be a problem. If you also have borrowing capacity in an existing business, you may be able to borrow against the strength of that, particularly since the profit stream in the new business could stand a little more interest, but you're unlikely to be able to finance the full amount this way, since the profit stream and cash flow of the new business clearly could not stand additional borrowing of another £287,000. You're therefore forced into providing some of the money yourself in cash (which most financiers would feel more comfortable with anyway) and/or raising equity. If you have the full £287,000 available, well and good. All you need to decide is whether the business and your plans for it will generate adequate returns on that sum. If you don't have enough, you're forced to consider selling some of the shares in the business. And then, as they say, you're in a whole new ball park.

The difference between asking a financier for a loan and asking him to put equity into your business is a matter of risk. If your business proves to be a disastrous failure, the lender should be in a position to get his money back so long as it is secured on the assets of the business. Not so the equity financier. He is likely to be putting money into the business without the benefit of security and he, like you, is a shareholder who will come bottom of the list in the event of the company having to be wound up. Consequently, he will look much more closely at you when putting money in and is likely to take more of a continuing interest. The proposal that you get from such a financier is likely to require that he receive at least some of his money back over a period of time and that some of it carry a dividend. However, it is normal for some of his money to be put in in the form of ordinary shares similar to your own. Consequently, he ends up owning part of the business in precisely the same way as you own the rest of it.

In addition to looking at the return which you will be paying the equity financier on some of his money, there is one other fundamental consideration to take into account: what proportion of your company will you have to part with in order to raise the sum you need? Equity investors look normally to receiving between 15 and 45 per cent of the company for their money. They almost never look for more than 50 per cent but your interest will, in general, be best served by minimising the percentage stake taken by the investor.

Going back to the example mentioned earlier, any offer of equity finance which you get is likely to be based on the historical profitability of the company and the profitability which you can convince the investor that you will be able to generate in the future. You bought the company at a price based on its past income stream and (presumably) the vendor's perception of what it might do in the future. If you want to get a better price for the piece of it which you are selling on, you have to convince your financier that the income stream will improve with you in the driving seat.

Taking the simplest of views, the income stream has been rising at £10,000 per year for the last two years. At £500,000, you have purchased the business at a cost of 3.33 × its most recent pre-tax profit (£150,000). If you can present the financier with proposals which convince him you can raise that profitability to £250,000 within the next three years and sell to him on the same multiple, you immediately raise the capital to £833,000 in his eyes. Even if you need to raise the whole £287,000 in this way, you will still have to part with only around 35 per cent of the business in order to get the money (ie £287,000 as a percentage of £833,000 is 34.4 per cent).

Let it be emphasised that arriving at this kind of bargain can involve a long and tortuous process of negotiation and you will usually be well advised to seek professional help while going through it. But, in principle, the above is essentially what is involved. In addition, just stop and consider for a moment what you would have achieved in this case. You would have purchased a profitable company by borrowing on the strength of its own assets and raising equity on its own future potential income stream; all you have to provide is that vital expertise needed to generate that increase in income. In terms of hard cash, it's cost you little and in some cases nothing at all, and a case such as this is by no means atypical.

Motivating the staff

It's highly unlikely that you'll be able to achieve a significant increase in profitability in any business, new or existing, on your own. Considerable emphasis has already been placed in this book on the importance of people and, if anything, that importance is heightened when a business changes hands. It's quite probable that when you acquire a company there will be people already working for it whom you would like to keep in place and whom you would like to motivate to contribute to improved performance. People are motivated in different ways (some by security, some by status, some by money etc) and your first task is to get to know your key people and establish exactly what it is that they want out of life. It's likely that the individuals who contribute most significantly to generating income will be financially motivated in some way. However, the days when we thought we could make people perform better merely by throwing more money at them are mercifully passing and you have to realise that getting the best results out of them can be quite a sophisticated business.

In an economic climate which emphasises the virtues and values of wealth, self-employment and company ownership, more and more people would like to be able to take a stake in the company which they work for. A change of ownership can be a good opportunity to make appropriate arrangements for key people. Interestingly, the stake you give people need not be large in order to motivate and if you set up a share option scheme, you don't have to part with shares in the first instance at all.

Such a scheme works by granting an employee the option to buy shares in the company at a future date but at their present day value. There exist certain tax-efficient means which imply minimal tax costs to the employee for participating in the scheme (which, of course, means that you really need the help of an experienced accountant to set the scheme up). The employee then has the right to subscribe for the shares (a maximum of 10 per cent of the company's value) at some time between three and ten years from the date of grant of the option. Hopefully, the effective cost to you of granting the option is nil, since you would expect the value of the company to rise by more than the value of the option in the intervening period. In addition, the obvious benefit to you, the employer, is not only the motivation which the option brings but also the fact that key employees become tied to the company which means you can be confident of retaining your most important people.

Motivation, however, means different things to different people. The key manager who will give his all if he has a stake in the company may be totally unmoved by quarterly bonuses or a bigger car. The salesman who wouldn't look twice at a share option scheme might easily be stimulated by the carrot of a holiday contingent upon achieving targets. Administrators who are motivated by security may want no more than praise and appreciation which follows through into a reasonable annual pay rise.

Motivation should start with knowing clearly what kind of people you need to carry out a particular function within an organisation. It needs to continue with locating and employing that type of person. Why? Because square pegs in round holes will never be happy and unhappy people never work effectively. Make people feel good about themselves and what they do and half the motivational battle is over. Then, and only then, is it worth giving detailed thought to the kind of incentives which will make people perform better.

Summary

1. Generic growth is the normal route forward for most companies. Only when it does not provide the growth factor which you are looking for should you turn to the idea of acquisition.

2. You may, however, wish to consider acquisition for a number of reasons such as availability of time, lack of expertise, to gain an introduction into a market, to obtain a client list or to obtain assets.

3. Having determined at the strategic level the need for an acquisition, you will next need to turn your attention to locating an acceptable target.

4. If that target is already on the market, it is vital to consider why the vendor is selling and whether his reason is also the very reason why you should not buy it.

5. Establishing a price should not be a matter of taking the vendor's figure and trying to beat him down. Start by considering in detail what the business ought to be worth to you; take the initiative and minimise the price.

6. Having established with the vendor an acceptable price in principle, determine how the purchase will be financed. If you cannot furnish the whole of the purchase price from your own resources, consider first borrowing against the assets of the company you are buying. Thereafter, if necessary, look to selling equity in the business.

7. The above is a complex, time-consuming and vital process. If you need professional advice, do not be afraid to use it.

8. An acquired business will be worth nothing to you if the people you employ are not motivated. Start by ensuring that you have the right people in the right jobs and then establish what will encourage them to work best.

Chapter 9
Getting There

There is only point in taking action in business: if that action has, or is expected to have, a desired consequence. You're not in business merely for the pleasure of doing things, so don't be afraid to question your own and other people's actions. The benefits of some actions may not be tangible and they may not be quantifiable either, but they should certainly be definable. Simply because corporate planning may be a fairly new and alien idea to you, does not mean that it is exempt from the logical enquiry that should govern all business actions.

The thinking outlined above should not cause too many arguments, since it's pure common sense to expect results. But in the final event, how many businessmen sit down and analyse *past* actions to establish whether they achieved desired results or if they didn't, to find out why not? Applying the question to the corporate planning process, you start on the assumption that you engaged in corporate strategy in order to maximise your chances of getting your business from A to B. At what point is it appropriate to sit down and determine whether you have succeeded and if not, why not? Or to put the question in another way:

What period should the planning process cover?

The first answer is that the industry you are in will determine the most appropriate length of the overall cycle. It is common knowledge that oil companies set horizons 50 years or more into the future and there are a number of other industries in which companies should be doing the same but aren't. Conversely, those in industries which fluctuate over much shorter cycles (fashion, tourism etc) may be disinclined to try to plan strategically at all. But for most industries, even for those with extreme cycles, there should be a happy medium and experience in most fields tends to suggest that around five years is normally optimal. Go much longer and most people can't cope with the personal implications. Go much shorter and you're unlikely to be planning strategically at all. For those with very long cycles, while it's possible to plan in general terms much further ahead, it becomes increasingly difficult to establish specific targets as you make the time-scales longer. In the shorter cycled industries, while there is clearly a need to formulate detailed plans over the natural cycle, if you don't go further and plan strategically, you are in danger of losing control over the direction of the business as a whole.

However, there are two key dangers of devising plans over five-year periods. The first is that everyone knuckles down to the job of planning just to humour the boss and when the process is over, the plan is thankfully consigned to the bottom drawer and forgotten. At the other extreme, the second danger is that once finished, the plan becomes carved in tablets of stone and no matter what fortunes the future may bring, the company stays rooted to its original strategy however inappropriate. It goes without saying that neither response is satisfactory. The only way to make the five-year plan work for you (instead of you working for the plan) is to treat it as a working, living document. As a working document, it has given you only a definition of where you are now, a set of targets to work to and a relatively broadly defined route for getting to those targets. To be of any practical use, it must, therefore, be followed by a more detailed, shorter-term operational plan.

The concept of short-term operational planning does not fall within the parameters of this book. However, it suffices to say that, in the context of a five-year strategic plan, operational planning should ideally commence with a three-year marketing plan whose objectives are set as the strategies defined within the strategic plan. This, in turn, will have direct implications for other operational areas of the business (production, financing, sourcing etc) and ultimately will devolve into a series of annual budgets. Of course, at any stage, the conclusions reached may have implications for the objectives set at the previous planning level. It must, therefore, be possible where necessary to modify the strategic plan in light of the practical requirements it places on running the business. Indeed, it is only if this approach of testing the plan against reality is taken that it will be possible to use the plan effectively as a working document.

If the plan is to 'live' it must not only change in the light of planning decisions further down the process, it must also be regularly reviewed and revised in the light of the changing internal and external environment as well. The best way to ensure that it stays relevant is to hold regular and fairly frequent planning meetings (quarterly is normally about right) whose brief is to ensure that either the company stays on course or that the course itself is deliberately and consciously modified. The commitment to the process may sound high but unless it is total, it will not have the chance to succeed. Having put so much time and effort into arriving at a workable planning document, it simply isn't worth risking the possibility of failure through devoting inadequate time and commitment to its success. And while we're on the subject . . .

Why might the plan fail and what do you do if it does?

The easiest answer to give is that it is never the plan that fails. Either the company fails to reach a target it should have achieved, or it fails to perceive early enough that the target is inappropriate and needs modification. If you want to understand failure in corporate planning you have, therefore, to start from the premise that it's no good blaming the plan. However, failures do and will continue to occur and to minimise their occurrence it's important to understand the nature of the reasons for failure.

These reasons can be grouped into three categories:

1. Failure to set the objective correctly.
2. Failure to modify the objective in the light of changing experience.
3. Failure to execute the actions necessary in order to achieve the objectives.

The first two are examples of failure in the planning process itself. In case 1 the fault lies at the heart of the process, in the definition of where the company is now and where it can realistically be by the end of the plan. Faults can arise in this area either through insufficient time being taken over understanding the present situation of the company or, having correctly understood the situation, in failure to set realistic targets. If, for either reason, you end up setting targets which simply are not appropriate, there is really only one solution: go back to the drawing board, find out where you're wrong, put your misunderstanding right and reset the objectives. These objectives can be wrong in two ways: they've either been set too low or too high (the amazing logic of corporate planning stuns us once again!), and the tendency in either case is to overreact. If you're committed to a target which is just too far above your head, the temptation is to respond by resetting it at a level you will find easy to achieve next time around. The inevitable then happens – you over-achieve, get fed up with this whole unworkable idea of corporate planning and go back to crisis management, having discredited the process in your own thinking. It all goes to emphasise just how crucial that first step is of getting the definitions right and setting the objectives at the right level in the light of those definitions.

It has been stressed throughout this book that corporate planning does not amount to crystal ball gazing. The value of the process lies in the global framework it allows you to create for taking tactical and operational decisions. Accordingly, if you expect to be able to predict the future from it you can also expect to be disappointed. To be useful at any other time than day one, the plan must be constantly reviewed and, where necessary, modified in the light of experience. Thus, at each review, the success you have had operationally within the strategic framework must be considered and new strategic decisions taken in the light of unforeseen circumstances which now prevail. The second category of failure arises either when you feel too committed to the plan to change it or you fail to see the need to carry on taking the strategic view as time passes.

Finally, you may be in the position of having set appropriate objectives, having modified them as necessary and yet still fail to achieve them. The failure here is operational. Congratulations – you got the strategy right! But something in the process of execution of that strategy went wrong. Undoubtedly, this can be the most difficult area in which to fall down, because defining the problem can be so difficult. Locating and correcting that problem can be one of the most complex and time-consuming exercises you will undertake. Unfortunately, it's unlikely to be a matter of taking the accounts, seeing that sales didn't perform and kicking the relevant manager. The difficulty may, in truth, lie in a wholly different area. But find it you must or you will have a permanent and irresolvable problem on your hands. In fact, it's probably one situation where you could rely heavily on your friendly management consultant; the objective independent eye is likely to spy the problem which you may miss.

While failure to achieve strategic objectives may be frustrating, it can be made to work for you. Look at your failures with the same analytical eye which you applied to devising the strategy in the first place, because to do so reinforces that mode of thinking. Additionally, periodically the plan will come in for major revision and at that stage you should be able to build in all you have learned from your shortcomings first time around.

What happens at the end of the plan?

The first question to ask here is whether you ever actually get to the end of the planning period at all. Certainly, if you set five-year objectives, have no cause to modify them along the way, derive successful operational plans and annual budget, you will get to the end of the period. If this should happen it is no great problem to make the process happen again for the next five years. However, life isn't usually quite like that for two reasons. First, the strong likelihood is that you will be modifying and fine-tuning the strategy at regular intervals along the way as discussed above. Second, there is a lot to be said for undertaking major revisions annually, with a further year being added to the plan as each year passes. The major advantage that such an approach brings is that you always have a five-year time horizon to work to. As you pass through each year of the plan, with the objectives being modified, it becomes considerably easier to set longer-term goals in the light of your experience in achieving the targets which you have previously set.

A rolling plan, therefore, has clear advantages over a static plan whose horizon draws ever closer. But if you are to adopt such an approach, one word of warning – it does not remove the need to ask, at each major review, the three key questions on which the strategic approach is based:

- Where are we now?
- Where do we want to be?
- How do we intend to get there?

Without these questions you don't have strategic planning at all, just five-year budgeting at best.

Planning and the changing economic environment

Finally, it's necessary to consider one further area which is not so much to do with 'getting there' as with the concept of corporate planning in its totality. What is, or should be the impact of the general economic cycle of activity on the strategic planning process?

Corporate planning is about the setting of strategic objectives towards which a company is intended to move over a period of time. Those objectives and the strategy for reaching them, must be constantly monitored and modified in the light of experience. Consequently, the emphasis is always placed on long-term objectives within the context of which short-term actions can be taken. There is, however, a strong temptation to look at general economic forces beyond the control of the company as being an influence so dominant as to make strategic planning pointless.

The logic applied is along the lines of: 'We can't be confident that the economy overall will go in any particular direction and economic forces are significant enough to render our planning meaningless. Therefore, why bother to plan at all?' Such an approach misses two points of fundamental importance.

Firstly, corporate strategy is about an attitude to management which lays emphasis on controlling a business, rather than being controlled by it. It is emphatically not about predicting the future. Consequently, the unpredictability of overall economic forces is not of commanding significance as long as you do not try to take the 'tablets of stone' approach to the corporate plan. In addition, in the context of the main corporate plan, it is always wise to have a contingency plan in reserve for the times when things don't work out as expected.

Second, while the timing of the economic cycle may be unpredictable, the fundamental fact that the economy moves in cycles and not in straight lines is indisputable. Unfortunately, memories tend to be short and after a few years of recession or a few years of growth, people start to believe that the world will never change. Now there isn't much in the corporate planning field that is predictable but one certain thing is that whatever the economic environment is at the time you commence the process, you can be sure that at some point in the future it is going to change.

The most important piece of advice that you can offer a corporate planner looking at the economic environment is to plan

141

for change, not consistency. However, the real difficulty, of course, is timing the changes. And determining the likelihood of substantial change within the planning horizon is an admittedly difficult task. To the extent that it truly has a bearing on your strategy, the best you can do is keep aware of all the information produced by central government and statistical agencies on the subject of cycles and order your thinking in the context of the predictions which are made.

Unfortunately, however, life is not always that simple. It's said that if you put five economists in a room with a problem they'll come out with six solutions. Put them in a room with statistical data and they'll probably come out with seven economic forecasts! Certainly, there will never be agreement among economists and analysts and at the time of writing, views range from, 'We're well into recovery' to, 'A 1930s style depression is imminent.' Not surprisingly, they can't all be right so whom do you believe? The answer is unsatisfactory: you simply have to weigh up the evidence for yourself and take a view. You may not end up with the right answer, but monitoring of the strategy should take care of your errors. The alternative, not planning at all, is really no alternative to the ambitious company set on going for growth.

It is important, however, not to get the economic background out of perspective. For most companies, it should be quite possible to trade profitably whatever the economic environment so long as the strategy is right. Indeed, unless you are an industry giant, the overall economic context ought not to be of fundamental importance. So long as your actions do not impact substantially on the market, it should be quite possible for you to grow by acquisition of market share when all around you are contracting.

Choose your industry right. Choose your sector right. Choose your product right. Choose your strategy right. Corporate, strategic planning for growth is about creating the long-term view, cultivating a forward thinking culture in the mind of a company in the context of which the right short-term decisions can be taken. You won't get it right all the time, so 'weaklings need not apply'. But for the company destined for the top, for the board going for growth, no matter what size, the only serious way forward is long-term, corporate, strategic planning.

Appendices

Appendix 1
Footloose Limited: An Approach to Corporate Planning

Footloose Limited is a commodity merchant based in the industrial Midlands. It was established in 1970 by the chairman at the age of 50 and by two of his three sons. After a lifetime spent working in the industry he perceived an opportunity to exploit a small segment of the market that was being inadequately addressed by the manufacturers – small-scale supply and prompt response times to small users of the product. Accordingly, Footloose Limited was born as a stockholder of the commodity, finding its niche in the market-place by buying in reasonable quantity from the manufacturers, stockholding and supplying small users quickly in a market that was traditionally used to long lead times. The company was founded from the start on the dual objectives of supplying quality products only and servicing the customers efficiently. Thus, the reputation of a high quality specialist supplier was quickly established.

Added to hard work and expertise, the company benefited from good fortune over the following 14 years. The particular segment of the market targeted grew rapidly as users of the product (who applied subsequent processes to it) increasingly demanded the ability to buy in the quantities they needed and be supplied quickly. Footloose rode the crest of the wave until in 1984 it turned over in excess of £8 million. Rapid growth was therefore something that the board (which by that time also included the chairman's third son) had come to expect.

But about this time three developments took place that set a different complexion on the future. First, industry surveys began to indicate that Footloose's segment of the market was now mature and was likely to grow at an annual rate of only 2 per cent. Footloose was one of two significant producers in the industry, implying that the theft of market share from other stockholders would be difficult and would certainly prompt retaliatory responses. Second, a smaller competitor in a slightly different segment of the industry came on the market. Third, now in his mid 60s, the chairman decided it was time for him to retire to a non-executive role.

The decision was taken to acquire the competitor since this would permit both the continued expansion of the company over the next 18 months and the ability to offer customers a broader range of service. The chairman's retirement meant that one son took on the managing director's role as well as continuing to wear the sales director's hat. The other two formalised their roles as works and finance directors respectively. While this dealt effectively with any serious problem on retirement and while the growth problem was dealt with temporarily, it was clear that the potential climacteric would have to be addressed shortly. The company successfully absorbed its new acquisition and the chairman happily retired to a non-executive place on the board. All appeared well, other than the fact that each of the directors felt too busy to sit back and take an overall view of the company as a whole.

By 1986 it had clearly become necessary to address the question of the future of the company, particularly in view of the impending decline of the growth rate. Accordingly, a specialist management consultant was called in to add the objective perspective that the board felt they lacked. The consultant started the exercise by spending a day with the whole board discussing three questions:

- What was the company about and why was it successful?
- Where did the directors want to be in five years?
- What were the main problems currently facing it?

Thereafter he went on to spend time with each of the directors individually considering their current and future roles within the company. In addition he held interviews with key staff members to gain a perspective on the company that was not available at board level. Following this, a further period of discussion with the board corporately was held to consider findings and possible strategic objectives. The consultant would then write a corporate plan for the company which would go before the board for approval at a subsequent meeting.

Corporate and individual discussion revealed that the major problems had little to do with immediate future growth as highlighted originally by the board. Rather, there were other problems that had previously gone unidentified which were more fundamental to the future of the business. In particular it became clear that while the company's turnover and profitability had grown, its thinking had not. It was still run very much as a small company, with all significant operational decisions being taken at board level. This caused the dual problems of the directors having insufficient time to take the strategic view and frustration among the senior employees who were constrained from taking the responsibility that they wanted. The solution lay in each director making a conscious effort to delegate more to frustrated subordinates, and in several cases a change of role as well. The managing director was to give up wearing two hats, and the national sales manager was appointed sales director. The MD was charged with the responsibility of ensuring the implementation of the whole corporate plan, of being a fully operational managing director and undertaking a strategic study of future opportunities for the company.

Various other significant changes completed the package which was presented verbally to the board on the final operational day of the exercise. The recommendations were thoroughly discussed, and their implications for the company and each director considered in detail. Each was charged with certain special responsibilities in relation to the plan and target dates set for achievement. A written document was produced and presented to the board for final approval which was given several weeks later. Finally, the non-executive chairman was given overall responsibility for seeing that each director and the board as a whole undertook the action to which it had committed itself. The plan was used thereafter to monitor progress on a quarterly basis, and it was clearly understood all round that it would have to be modified and updated regularly in the light of changing circumstances.

Appendix 2
W A Webb Group: A One-Year Plan

The text that follows is a verbatim representation of a one-year plan written entirely by the chairman of a group of building companies, Mr W A Webb. It is presented without any comment, other than that it exemplifies perfectly what can be achieved with the discipline of the strategic approach and a little assistance in understanding how that approach can be used. It should be read as what it is meant to be: a one-year operational plan and not a five-year strategic plan.

<u>W A WEBB BRICKWORK LIMITED</u>
<u>W A WEBB BUILDERS LIMITED</u>

<u>A ONE-YEAR PLAN</u>

Instigated by the Dale Carnegie Management Course
1 December 1985

Foreword

This document represents the requirements of the Dale Carnegie Management Course as an exercise but also incorporates the realities of my companies' actual position and future plans.

In the report I have attempted to analyse my current position, set a goal of where I wish to be in one year and my intended actions or instigations in between. Whenever possible the reasons for those actions and instigations are also laid down, so as to form an integral part of the report for later evaluation or change, should it prove helpful or necessary.

The report, although my first step in planned management by recognised methods and rules, has been of incalculable value to me in its preparation. The concept of planning a strategy over one year would never have been instigated, nor its undoubted rewards made obvious, had it not been for my enrolment on to the above course. For this I shall always be grateful.

W A W CHAIRMAN

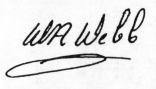

Quote on strategy

It is an obvious statement that during the Falklands crisis, as with any war, the success of our troops was not based on some vague, undefined, stumbling, random deployment of resources. The victory was gained because a clear strategy was formulated, troops and machines were deployed in set ways at certain times to maximum advantage. That does not mean that every bullet found its mark, nor even that every skirmish was successful – but in order to raise the flag of success there had to be strategy. Without strategy there would have been certain defeat.

Quote on objectives

This is also crucial. Without objective we never function at our best. Our objective is not just immediate new business, as most of us need that and it must therefore form part of our strategy. The main objective is to pursue successfully a course of action that will change prospects for the future and form qualitative long-term relationships with staff and clients which will inevitably bring the on-going business success required. (Extracts borrowed from a sales training course)

W A Webb conclusion

Our strategy must be a series of pre-planned steps which enable us to realise our objectives.

The major goal

To oversee the successful transfer of my companies to a broader base with a large turnover, while maintaining their present efficiency and profitability together with their current high quality staff. This accomplished a complete change in direction on a scale to enhance new ideas after proper planning and investigation so as to add to the success of the companies for the future.

The companies' current particulars – 1.12.85

W A Webb Brickwork Limited

Brickwork and Carpentry Contractors
Turnover: 1.3 million pa
Profitability: Gross 27%   Nett 13%
Staff: 1 Office Secretary
                1 Senior Contracts Manager
                1 Assistant Contracts Manager – Part-time
                1 Senior Contracts Surveyor
                1 Assistant Contracts Surveyor
                1 Estimator
                1 YTS (in Estimating Department)
    TOTAL   6+
Office: 13 Bellevue Road
                City Centre
                Southampton
                Hampshire
                Tel: Southampton 36525

Employees and Sub-Contractors – 100/150 men
75% Self Employed but working for an hourly rate
25% Self Employed on a sublet price

Period of Training – 13 years

Bankers: Barclays Bank plc
                50 Jewry Street
                Winchester
                Hampshire

W A Webb Builders Limited

Maintenance and Building Contractors
Turnover: 800,000 pa
Profitability: Gross 27%   Nett 13%
Staff: 1 Office Secretary
                1 Senior Contracts Supervisor
                1 Assistant Contracts Supervisor – Part-time
                1 Senior Contracts Surveyor
                1 Assistant Contracts Surveyor
                1 Estimator
    TOTAL   6
Office: 6 Portersbridge Street
                Romsey
                Hampshire
                Tel: Romsey 522285

Employees and Sub-Contractors – 40/50 men
90% Self Employed on a sublet price
10% Self Employed but working on an hourly rate

Period of Training – 2 years

Bankers: Bank of Scotland
148 High Street
Southampton

General set-up at present

W A Webb's Conference Portakabin
The Builders Yard
6 Portersbridge Street
Romsey
Hampshire

Managing Director, Company Manager, 1 Wages Clerk, 1 Computer Programmer, 1 Office Manager – Part-time.

The above operate between both offices stated also and are mostly costed to the Brickwork Company.

NB. The above companies have a good name in the trade and are very experienced in labour control which is predominantly their business.
There is no overdraft in any of the above companies.

Office set-up

At today's date the company operates from three sets of offices.

1. 13 Bellevue Road, City Centre, Southampton (BRICKWORK)
2. 6 Portersbridge Street, Romsey   (BUILDERS)
3. Portakabin, Portersbridge Street, Romsey   (HOLDINGS)

THE REASONS FOR THE ABOVE ARE:

1. Bellevue Road offices were not large enough to include Building Company when it was formed.
2. W A Webb personally owned Portersbridge Street offices so the Building Company utilised them.
3. Due to lack of offices W A Webb operates uninterrupted in the Portakabin at Portersbridge Street, Romsey.

THIS CAUSES THE FOLLOWING PROBLEMS:

1. Lack of central control in general office procedure.
2. Jobs being unnecessarily duplicated.
3. Extra non-visible charges occurring.
4. Management cannot always be on hand when required.
5. Travelling times between offices are lost needlessly.
6. The central core of control is by definition split.
7. There is no room for expansion in any of the above should it become necessary.

REMEDIES REQUIRED TO RECTIFY THE SITUATION:

Relocation

1. Relocation into one unit of offices large enough to cope with the current permanent staff but with enough space to expand if necessary.

Company power base

At today's date the company operates almost entirely on a labour base, supplying and controlling a large workforce currently to two major companies only.

THE REASONS FOR THE ABOVE ARE:

1. This was the industry first entered.
2. Success at the above has obviously been achieved.
3. The scope to enlarge has been available.
4. The area into which the Building Company has made inroads contractually-wise has been because of our ability to suply and control labour.
5. The profits it has generated relative to the capital employed have been excellent.

THIS CAUSES THE FOLLOWING PROBLEMS:

1. It is a shrinking market on the Brickwork side due to the economic reality of 'going for the cheapest price', therefore specialist labour becomes less saleable at 'our price'.
2. To maintain company structure, smaller profits have to be taken, equalling large turnover to maintain status quo. This eventually requires higher numbers to control, which in reality equals ever-rising spiral with profits shrinking almost permanently.
3. The competitors in Brickwork are progressively more informed and numerous.
4. With regard to the Builders, problems are not at this stage obvious, other than increased competition due to other contractors applying to tender for contracts we would like to be considered for.
5. Plus the inability to enlarge our operation to other local authorities due to today's lack of experience.

REMEDIES TO CORRECT THE SITUATION:

Broaden power base

Attempt to maintain the status quo within the existing managerial framework as far as the Brickwork Company is concerned. Form an aggressive marketing policy to forward the name of the Building Company with the intent of being asked to tender on more council work. Broaden the base of the work being sought at the same time as the above and actively seek more clients to spread the dependence factor.

Planning for the future

At yesterday's date the companies had never had nor operated any type of formula on plans for the future.

THE REASONS FOR THIS ARE:

1. I was unaware of the term 'corporate plan'.
2. Consequently I was unaware of its necessity.
3. Nobody in our companies' management had stressed the importance of a corporate plan.
4. Everything seemed to grow regularly even though it was not planned.

THIS CAUSES THE FOLLOWING PROBLEMS:

1. Everybody is involved only in 'doing the job'.
2. No planning means lots of time spent in 'spare moments' being given to very important tasks.
3. Always having to improvise, not just in emergencies but on a day-to-day basis.
4. 'Planning' as it was called actually was only to do with running problems, not future requirements, resulting in a 'locked-in attitude'.
5. Growth with no plans set out meant that all aspects of expansion were immediate and consequently more disorganised and costly.
6. The lack of a financial based, forward-facing plan meant the costs of growth could only be 'valued' after the fact, many times to be to the companies' misfortune.

REMEDIES TO CORRECT THE SITUATION:

Corporate plan
Set out a completely new set of guidelines against which the current day-to-day activities can be measured and checked. This done, would create a formula and framework within which 'planning' becomes a vital cog, not just a part; always remember the adage: *'THAT TRUE SUCCESS IS NEARLY ALWAYS PLANNED'*

Senior management structure

At today's date the companies operate in line with the structured plan attached to the Companies' Current Particulars Schedule.

THE REASONS FOR THIS STRUCTURE ARE:

1. The rapid growth of 'Builders' not being planned.
2. The need to 'get the job done' meant structuring as quickly as possible with that in mind.
3. Unawareness of the requirements necessary to meet the challenge of any further growth.
4. Management experience in our growth situation was found to be short on the ground.

THIS CAUSES THE FOLLOWING PROBLEMS:

1. It is totally incorrectly structured from a management point of view.
2. The company manager cannot possibly cope with future workload or planning because he is too busy trying to manage successfully.
3. When he (the company manager) is not around there are no other areas of control (only reliability factors).
4. *Effective* day-to-day control can be lost because of the two companies' different requirements of its one manager.
5. The growth so far has meant some staff are in the wrong position or title.

REMEDIES TO CORRECT THE SITUATION:

Restructure
A complete company restructure of its staff and positions relative to effective day-to-day control *and* future requirements whether by promotion or recruitment from 'outside', forming a properly constituted management structure, not present today.

Paperwork systems

As at today's date the company copes reasonably well with paperwork systems, either invented from within or acquired from new members of staff over the years. These systems are as set out below:

W A W Brickwork and W A W Builders

1. Weekly payment schedule – (value of work done) monthly and quarterly.
2. Weekly site cost analyst – (value of site costs) monthly and quarterly.
3. Monthly accounts and staff costs – quarterly.
4. Weekly – monthly – quarterly profit and loss based on the above.
5. Monthly cash flow (actual but one month in arrears).
6. Monthly cash flow (forecast for next six months).

THE REASONS FOR THE ABOVE:

1. To help a very tight and reasonably accurate check on cost to value in each week.
2. To keep an accurate analysis of the monthly cost and value.
3. To keep a flowing record of quarterly costs and values to be used (in conjunction with the above) for ascertaining trends, peaks or troughs, also for analysing with regard to future planning.

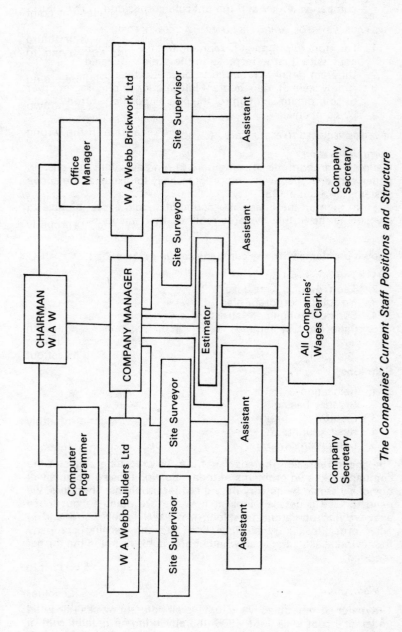

The Companies' Current Staff Positions and Structure

4. To keep abreast of the *actual* cash flow position of the companies today and the anticipated position in the future.

THIS CAUSES THE FOLLOWING PROBLEMS IN A GROWTH POSITION:

1. Far more information is required but the old situation cannot cope with a large increase in the scale requested.
2. Different detail is required to plan effectively.
3. A new level of management information is required in order to co-ordinate and control the overall position currently split by companies.

REMEDIES REQUIRED TO RECTIFY THE SITUATION:

Computerisation
Instigate a programme of computers to run pay-roll to the existing paperwork and effectively and progressively to take over the above systems by 1 June 1986.

From then on the financial accountant should in fact be able to investigate the further systems required by management.

Known problems with the company set-up as described:

1. The office set-up
2. The type of power base
3. No future corporate plan
4. Senior management structure
5. Paper-work systems

Solutions

1. Relocation
2. Broader basing
3. Plan for the future
4. Restructuring
5. Computerisation

The above represent the answers from the preceding pages of the companies' known problems of today. Solving those problems will obviously create by its very nature further problems. Therefore, we need to take a detailed look at how we are going to put these answers into operation, how long it is likely to take, how and in what order to plan their inception into the existing company framework. Lastly, the cost, whether affordable or not in the format required.

1. Relocation

The major current objective is to have all different offices relocated under one roof by 1 June 1986, thereby bringing greater control and more efficiency, together with less cost to the company. It will also assist in the 'controlling' of the growth anticipated.

PROBLEMS AND REQUIREMENTS ASSOCIATED WITH RELOCATION

1. Suitable office accommodation has to be found, bought or built by 1 May 1986.
2. A date of 1 June 1986 for the 'actual' physical relocation be fixed so as to minimise disruption. Moving all existing furniture etc over one weekend to join all extra furniture newly purchased and installed. All stationery, advertising, business cards, directory entries and standard letters are printed with the new address (possibly logos) plus telephone numbers one month prior to moving.
3. Arrangements for all mail and telephone calls to be redirected from the day of the move.
4. To ensure that everybody we work for, together with any other interested parties including the VAT and tax offices, are informed of the move a month in advance.
5. All new accounts necessary for office running in the new area to be opened.
6. To help and assist all current staff to our utmost when requesting the transfer to the new workplace.

The above deals with what we wish to do, the timetable envisaged and likely problems we must overcome.

The costing of this operation has to be dealt with under the Financial Strategy Plan which includes financing, taxation priorities and banking requirements. However, it should be noted that all in all the company cannot *afford* under any circumstances not to relocate under one roof. The only real question is, how far does 'if' go cost-wise.

2. Broader power base

The major current objective is successfully to hold our current turnover in the Brickwork Company. To increase our turnover on the Building Contract side and allowing for future growth within both companies if required. A broader base of clients is also a major current goal under this heading.

PROBLEMS AND REQUIREMENTS ASSOCIATED WITH POWER BASE ENLARGEMENT

1. Appoint a professional marketing company to advise on how to instigate an effective, aggressive marketing policy for the companies.
2. Assess the cost to benefit expectations.
3. According to cost, the formation of a planned Company Marketing Policy.
4. Actively instigate the above.
5. The purchasing or taking over of an existing established building contracting company (provided it is cost effective).
6. After purchasing another contracting company, a successful integration into our own existing structure within a short period is vital.

7. All or any of the above to be investigated before our relocation date of 1 June.

The above deals with what we wish to do, how we must pursue that goal and its timetable for implementation.

The actual costs of either of the two actions above are at this time non-determinable; however, it will be company policy to look at, evaluate and choose from as many options as possible, but by necessity be governed by the financial policy incorporated in the companies' final strategy plan.

3. Plan for the future

Companies' Policy on Planning
The major objective of the above is to be in some control of where we wish to be and how we wish to get there, as opposed to just arriving. For the current situation, it also incorporates knowing where we are today so as to judge the viability of the goals we set.

PROBLEMS AND REQUIREMENTS ASSOCIATED WITH FORMING A COMPANY
POLICY ON PLANNING

1. A framework to be set up in order to assess current and future workload requirements to overhead costs on a current basis.
2. The formation of a 'planning only' meeting once a month with senior management of both companies to carry out the above.
3. A cash flow broad-sheet to be introduced to show affordability of any schemes put forward at this initial stage.
4. The formation of a properly constituted, professionally advised company strategy policy.

4. Restructuring

Recruitment or Promotion of Key Staff
The major current objective is to monitor constantly the situation of key staff and their performance, also to analyse the expected requirements the future will demand of existing staff and their ability to adapt to those demands so as to progress as an asset to the company. Outside recruitment must take place in certain areas because of a general lack of management expertise at the top.

PROBLEMS AND REQUIREMENTS ASSOCIATED WITH RESTRUCTURING

1. A new company structured plan has to be formulated by the time we move to new offices.
2. I have to be aware of the requirements of all the positions which will be decided by the company structure.
3. The staff chosen are operating within their given defined position, results, descriptions within six months of promo-

tion or joining the company or of 1 June, whichever is sooner.

4. Their ability to innovate or add experience lacking within the company is noted within six months of joining the company or of their promotion.
5. The person proves his ability to delegate successfully and control effectively the direction of staff under his department, again within six months of joining the company or of their promotion.
6. To explain to our current workforce at supervising level the decisions made, the reasons for them and their place for the future.
7. The creation of a framework in management to observe individual aptitude for management and level of responsibility (ie for internal promotion responsibilities).

The above deals with what we wish to do and the time-scale envisaged for completion. The actual restructured plan with details of positions and responsibilities in general follows the financial aspect of restructuring and will be covered in the financial report.

5. Computerisation

The major objective is to have all the companies' existing and successfully working systems computerised, so as to allow the 'extra' workload (ie turnover etc) to be coped with as efficiently as today's, with the large company envisaged.

PROBLEMS AND BENEFITS ASSOCIATED WITH COMPUTERISATION

1. The main sections of wages-accounts-valuations of W A Webb Brickwork Limited running completely off computers successfully. This is to be achieved by March 1986.
2. The main sections of wages-accounts-valuations of W A Webb Builders Limited running completely off computers successfully. This is to be achieved by June 1986.
3. The two companies above are joined together by a third computer system to be used as a management tool for control, budgeting, forecasting, analysing and planning by December 1986.

The above deals with what we wish to do and the time-scale involved.

The costing of this operation has to be dealt with under the Financial Report. However, it should be noted that without the information level available to management, through computer, any company's growth would be severely held back.

Resume

The companies' current position and remedies, together with the timetable anticipated and most where known, can now be shown in the format required to incorporate into the one-to-three-year plan. The following are details which have to be incorporated to rectify the current position before future prospects can evolve under a *planned* format.

Relocation

Where	Owned land at Romsey – to be built by Builders.
When	A date of 1 June (installed) is of major importance.
How	Transfer operation planned and overseen by the current office manager.
Cost	Calculations to be assessed in financial report.

Broader basing

Where	All the literature, brochures and logos will of course be based with our new offices in mind.
When	From immediate instigation, six months can be spent putting the whole package together to coincide with the new offices being built.
How	Instigation of immediate enquiries to several major professional marketing companies to ascertain who will do the final completed plan etc.
Cost	Calculations to be assessed in the financial report.

Plan for the future

Where	Existing companies' structures and formats are to be agreed and put into operation.
When	As of February 1986 Planning Only Meetings will be held once a month with senior management and department heads.
How	A rough guide will be operated, although it will be in general tune with the requirements of the Companies' Corporate Structural Plan as a temporary measure.
Cost	This can only be ascertained as 'TIME' or time costs, (ie *IF IT IS NOT IMPLICATED*).

Restructuring

When	This will be started during January 1986 and completed by May 1986.
How	The structured format of the companies' staff position today will change in line with the dates given. The promotion or recruitment of key staff will take place along the lines shown with the recruitment of the position being identified with the appointment.
Cost	Calculations to be assessed in the financial report on all areas.

Computerisation

Where   To begin at the companies' present locations.
When   With immediate co-ordinated effect.
How   By qualified computer programmers.
Cost   Calculations to be assessed in the financial report.

Final structural analysis of implementing the one-year structure plan

Before the foregoing one-year plan was envisaged a certain proportion of forward planning on a rather *ad hoc* basis had been instigated.

All items mentioned in the foregoing pages were, in one form or another, currently under review. With the actual formation of the enclosed, the fitting together of the *ad hoc* thoughts with a set plan became somewhat easier than at first envisaged.

The *ad hoc* initial stages had included a review of the companies' resources in both finance and land. It was found to be advantageous to develop the existing land bank and utilising the after-sale proceeds for the development of new offices at 6 Portersbridge Street, Romsey, currently owned by the company. With the assistance of the company accountants and bankers, a format for financing the development projects was pieced together and in general terms accepted. The latter stage of planning consents was also tackled by way of an architect's appointment.

Since the instigation of the one-year plan I have endeavoured to turn the principles of the above into constructive format by way of clarifying all details, with the current position looking favourable from the planning department concerned.

With the company restructuring you will note that in the early stages the number of staff currently employed will not increase until March. Those then joining the company have been costed into the development at Portersbridge Street, (ie offices) and it is not until May that further management staff will affect current overhead expenditure.

With regard to computerisation, budgets had been set and allowed for the coming financial year. Early forms of computer packages had in fact been investigated and certain computer hardware purchased. With the instigation of the one-year plan the software required has now been identified and installed within the budget allowed. It is envisaged that the operators' costs, already accounted for in overhead evaluation, will successfully complete this task by May.

The marketing policy envisaged in the plan will be a cost of the company, as yet undetermined. It is conceivable that the budget allowing for the development of the company's land bank will allow a cost towards marketing the properties. It is therefore hoped that the 'extra costs' of setting up a *company marketing policy* can be offset to a level which would indicate usual anticipated advertisement requirement cost.

Finally, it should be noted from the one-year plan that the most activity takes place during the first six months.

There are two reasons for this:

1. As explained above, most changes had been instigated and tackled prior to the plan. These only required suitable impetus and direction to be given.

2. It is felt that the latter six months should be used to consolidate and evaluate all new management positions and to formulate a further one-year plan based on the success or otherwise of the one-year plan now completed.

Chairman/Managing Director

Through plans 1-5 the chairman and managing director's major current objective is effectively to control and liaise over all areas so far mentioned, with the goal of everyday management becoming efficient and supervised. Also to pursue actively future workload and represent the companies' interest as and when required.

Contracts Manager

The current plan now shows the demise of the title 'Company Manager'. This position will now be redefined and called 'Contracts Manager' with all that will entail.

The position benefits to the company

The major current objective is effectively to bring all the companies' existing site areas under one single control, whereby a better overall picture is formed, which in turn will assist in the expected companies' growth.

Chief Surveyor

Plan 1 shows the breakdown required by 1 February 1986.

This requirement is for a fundamental restructuring of the companies in general and for the bringing in of a Contracts Chief Surveyor. If this position is filled by the result of promotion, then a Senior Surveyor vacancy will have to be filled.

The position benefits to the company

Delegation of this specialist area from the existing management department has become essential.

Effective control of the various estimating and valuation departments within the organisation under one person.

Creates an extra tier of management to supply the greater scale of management information which could be required in a growth situation.

Allows for planned and continued growth without interference with the current workload or job allocations.

Senior Estimator/Senior Agent

Plan 2 shows the breakdown as required by 1 March. At this time there does not exist within the company management structure anyone who could be considered for promotion to this key area. The time-scale stated above allows those persons filling the vacancy to take overall control of the new office building project.

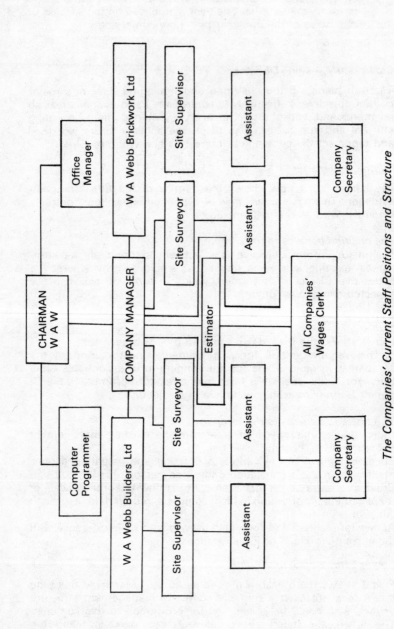

The Companies' Current Staff Positions and Structure

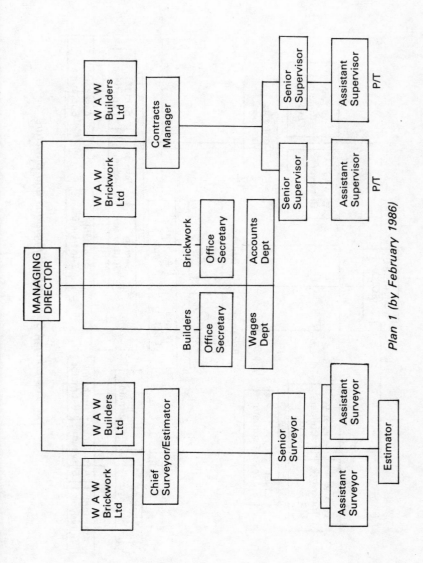

Plan 1 (by February 1986)

165

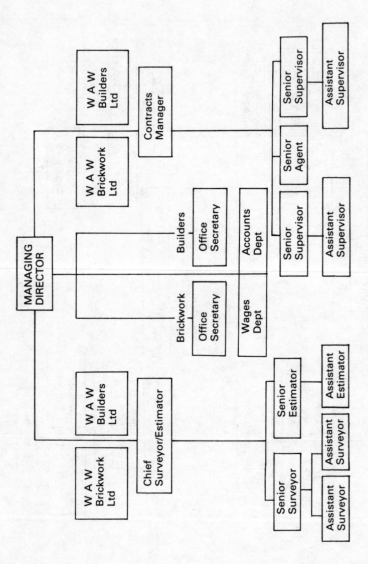

Plan 2 (by March 1986)

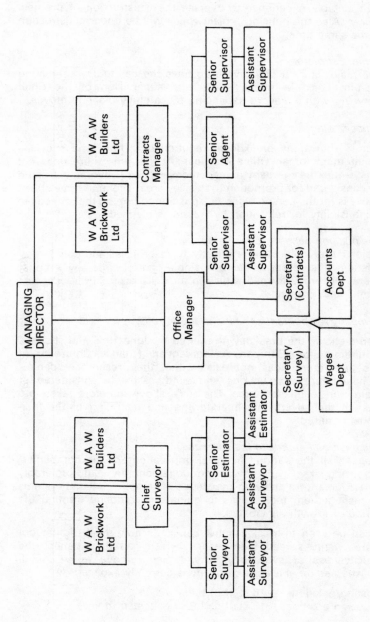

Plan 3 (by April 1986)

The position benefits to the company
The major current objective is to bring in a competent site agent with suitable experience to oversee the construction of the new offices. Also the housing project which will be under construction at the same time.

Senior Estimator
The major current objective is to have the day-to-day estimating brought back 'in house' under the supervision of the Chief Surveyor with a view to expanding by carefully planned moves.

Office Manager

Plan 3 shows the breakdown required by 1 April and shows a requirement for an Office Manager. At this time there does not exist within the company management structure anyone who could be considered for promotion to this key area. The time-scale stated above is for the person filling this position to take on the immediate responsibility for relocation by 1 June as planned.

The position benefits to the company
Major current objective is effectively to bring all the companies' existing office areas under one single control, whereby a better overall picture is formed, which in turn will assist in the expected companies' growth.

Company Accountant and Financial Controller

Plan 4 shows the breakdown required by June 1986 and shows a requirement for a Company Accountant and Financial Controller. At this time there does not exist within the present companies' management picture anyone who could possibly be considered for promotion to this key area. The scale above therefore takes into account the advertising, interviewing and recruiting of the individual required.

The position benefits to the company
Oversee all the various financial implications of the companies' increasing size. Giving advice and judgement, he would preferably be accountant-trained with knowledge of computer-related systems as management tools so as to guide our company through the period of growth anticipated.

It can be seen from plan 4 that control is now much tighter but more evenly spread than before, which can only benefit the effectiveness of everybody. It will also remove many inbuilt weaknesses to which the company is currently exposed.

Existing positions – 16 staff at today's date
Expected positions – 18 staff at 1.6.86 (2 costed to site)

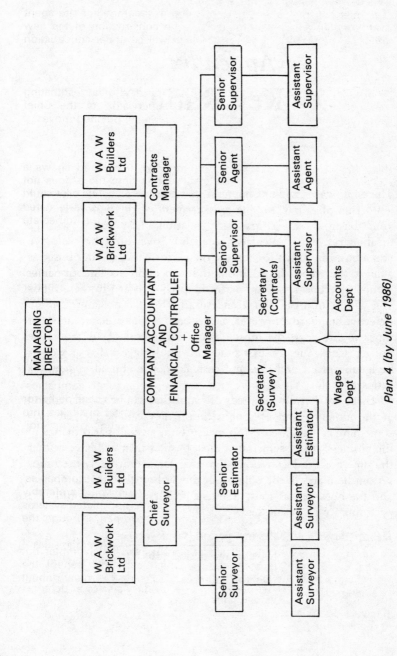

Plan 4 (by June 1986)

Appendix 3
Key Ratios

The point was raised in Chapter 5 that accounting ratios provide a good rule of thumb for the measurement of the performance of your business. Of course, in isolation these ratios will be meaningless, but if calculated frequently, over time they will give you a basis on which to measure the performance of your business against the trend. In addition, if it's possible to find out how comparable businesses are performing with regard to these ratios you will be in a position to measure performance against a more objective standard. However, as has been emphasised a number of times in this text, the most objective standard of all should be budget. Consequently, best practice would suggest that as well as budgeting profit and loss and cash flow, you should budget key ratios as well.

There are literally hundreds of ratios that can be calculated and at the ultimate level of sophistication they can be merged (into something called Z-scores) to measure the overall performance of the business. It is assumed that most businessmen will have neither the time nor the inclination to go that far. Accordingly the ratios set out here are, in the opinion of the author, the most important and the ones he has most frequent recourse to in measuring the performance of businesses.

Debtor days:
$$\frac{\text{Sales in a period (say 1 year)}}{\text{Days in the period (365)}} = \text{Average sales per day}$$

$$\frac{\text{Debtor balances}}{\text{Average sales per day}} = \text{Day's sales in debtors}$$

Creditor days:

$$\frac{\text{Purchases in a period (say 1 year)}}{\text{Days in the period}} = \frac{\text{Average}}{\text{purchases per day}}$$

$$\frac{\text{Creditor balances}}{\text{Average purchases per day}} = \frac{\text{Day's purchases}}{\text{in creditors}}$$

Stock turnover:

$$\frac{\text{Sales for the period}}{\substack{\text{Stock at period end} \\ \text{(valued at selling price)}}} = \frac{\text{Number of times}}{\substack{\text{stock turns over in} \\ \text{the period}}}$$

Liquidity:

$$\frac{\text{Net current assets}}{\text{Net current liabilities}}$$

or:

$$\frac{\text{Net current assets less stock}}{\text{Net current liabilities}}$$

Gross profit:

$$\frac{\text{Gross profit}}{\text{Turnover}} \times 100$$

Net operating profit:

$$\frac{\text{Net operating profit}}{\text{Turnover}} \times 100$$

Appendix 4
Going Public: The Flotation Option

The astute reader may have noticed an absence from the text of any reference to public flotation of the company as a corporate goal. This is essentially for two reasons: first, because though the Unlisted Securities Market seems to be flavour of the decade, the real value of a quote is strictly limited; second, public flotation and the wealth it brings may be an exciting personal target, but it is not a valid strategic corporate objective.

Going public is a very large, and effectively irreversible step. It is likely to be the biggest decision you will have faced since the inception of the business. But if, through the foregoing pages you have become convinced of the value of strategic planning, there is really only one way of looking at it: as a means of assisting in the achievement of specified corporate objectives. Accordingly, the decision to float or not to float (if indeed it is a feasible option) should only be taken in full knowledge of the advantages and disadvantages that it will bring and also in the knowledge that as capital markets become increasingly sophisticated, flotation is not the only possibility open to the entrepreneur who would like to capitalise on his success to date.

It is fair to point out however that of the 400 or so companies that, at the date of writing, have come to the USM, only a handful have expressed regret at doing so. As far as the others are concerned, it is impossible to say how many cases there are of ignorance being bliss. The principal advantages of coming to the market that are commonly expounded, together with some of the disadvantages, are listed briefly below. If the market is a future that you are considering, consult the experts and become as informed as possible. But before taking the plunge, remember two things:

- despite any protestations to the contrary, the experts expect to profit substantially from your flotation, so do not expect disinterested advice;
- at the end of the day it is your decision which should only be taken in the light of your clearly established corporate objectives.

Why you should go

1. Because it allows you to capitalise financially on your success to date. Surprisingly most directors of USM companies place this well down the list of reasons – can such an attitude be taken seriously?!
2. Because it brings considerable publicity – you decide whether this is good or bad. Certainly it can't be the only reason, since at a current minimim cost of not much less than £200,000, it's expensive publicity.
3. Because it's prestigious to be director of a PLC – certainly not a corporate objective, and can't you find a cheaper way of bolstering your self-esteem? However, the corporate prestige can be useful.
4. It gives you marketability of wealth. It provides you with a relatively easy route for disposing of further shares later – quite a reasonable point, this one.
5. It gets cash into the company. A very fair point this – flotation is likely to be the cheapest route if you need to get significant equity in, but do explore the other possibilities first. Loan capital may carry interest but at least you get to pay it off – not so with equity as someone else will always own a piece of your company. In addition there's now an active venture capital market in the UK which constitutes a viable alternative to flotation – do consider it even if you end up rejecting it.
6. It enables you to offer shares instead of cash for potential acquisitions. If you're acquisitive and not cash rich this can be quite an advantage.

Why you may not want to go

1. Because once you've done it it's virtually irreversible. If you don't like the heat once you're in you can't really get out of the kitchen, so make sure it's what you want before you commit yourself.

2. Because it exposes the company to the outside world in quite a new way. Think carefully whether you want the spotlight on you at a timing that may not be of your making.
3. Because your remuneration and perks may be limited. If you're used to very high salaries, pension contributions and company yachts think carefully whether the capital sum on the sale of shares is adequate compensation for losing them, because they may have to go.
4. Because it's an expensive process – a minimum of £200,000ish and rising at the time of writing. So if you're going to capitalise at less than £4 million forget it for now.

The message that should be coming across by now is 'don't overrate going public'. If it serves the corporate objectives and the advantages outweigh the disadvantages, fine. Otherwise find another way of doing what you want to do. And finally, don't don't don't look on it as an end in itself – if you do you'll be disappointed once you get there.

Index

INDEX